INTERNATIONAL CUISINE

INTERNATIONAL CUISINE
chicken & seafood

Sheila Davis
#2-267 Craig Street
Nanaimo, B.C. V9R 3V5
(250) 754-1485
Fax (250) 716-1754
E-mail: healthywealthyandwise@home.com
www.5pillars.com/sleeponit

JG
PRESS

Published by World Publications Group, Inc.
455 Somerset Avenue
North Dighton, MA 02764
www.wrldpub.net

All interior photographs courtesy of Sunset Books.
Cover photograph: ©Jonelle Weaver/Foodpix

ISBN 1-57215-452-7

Editors: Joel Carino and Emily Zelner
Designers: Lynne Yeamans and Stephanie Stislow
Production Director: Ellen Milionis

Printed and bound in China by SNP Leefung Printers Limited.

1 2 3 4 5   06 05 03 02

contents

chicken

chicken & snow peas

preparation time: about 45 minutes, plus 30 minutes to soak mushrooms

4 dried Asian mushrooms

2 teaspoons *each* soy sauce, cornstarch, dry sherry, and water

Dash of white pepper

1½ pounds chicken breasts, skinned, boned, and cut into bite-size pieces

3½ tablespoons salad oil

Cooking Sauce (recipe follows)

1 small clove garlic, minced or pressed

½ cup sliced bamboo shoots

¼ pound Chinese pea pods (also called snow or sugar peas) or sugar snap peas, ends and strings remove or 1 package (6 oz.) frozen Chinese pea pods, thawed and drained

1 Soak mushrooms in warm water to cover for 30 minutes, then drain. Cut off and discard stems; squeeze caps dry, thinly slice, and set aside.

2 In a bowl, mix soy, cornstarch, sherry, water, and white pepper. Add chicken and stir to coat, then stir in 1½ teaspoons of the oil. Let marinate for 15 minutes. Prepare Cooking Sauce; set aside.

3 Place a wok over high heat; when wok is hot, add 1 tablespoon of the oil. When oil begins to heat, add garlic and stir once. Add half the chicken mixture and stir-fry until meat is no longer pink in center; cut to test (about 3 minutes). Remove chicken from wok and set aside. Repeat to cook remaining chicken, adding 1 tablespoon more oil.

4 Pour remaining 1 tablespoon oil into wok. When oil is hot, add mushrooms and bamboo shoots. Stir-fry for 1 minute, adding a few drops of water if wok appears dry. Add pea pods and stir-fry for 3 minutes (30 seconds if using frozen pea pods), adding a few drops more water if wok appears dry. Return chicken to wok. Stir Cooking Sauce, pour into wok, and stir until sauce boils and thickens.

COOKING SAUCE

Stir together ½ cup water, 1 tablespoon dry sherry, 2 tablespoons oyster sauce or soy sauce, ¼ teaspoon sugar, 1 teaspoon sesame oil, and 1 tablespoon cornstarch.

makes 3 or 4 servings

per serving: 294 calories, 28 g protein, 12 g carbohyates,15 g total fat, 65 mg cholesterol, 604 mg sodium

macadamia chicken

preparation time: about 30 minutes

4 skinless, boneless chicken breast halves (about 1 lb. *total*)

1 piece pineapple (about 2 lbs.), peeled, cored, and cut crosswise into 4 equal slices

¼ cup Dijon mustard

3 tablespoons honey

1 tablespoon each salad oil and lime juice

2 packages (10 oz. *each*) frozen chopped spinach

2 tablespoons chopped salted macadamia nuts

Salt and pepper

1 Rinse chicken and pat dry. Place chicken (skinned side up) and pineapple side by side on rack of a 12-by 14-inch broiling pan. In a bowl, mix mustard, honey, oil, and lime juice; spoon half the mixture evenly over chicken and pineapple. Bake, uncovered, in a 450° oven until meat in thickest part is no longer pink; cut to test (about 20 minutes).

2 Meanwhile, cook spinach according to package directions; keep warm. Also warm remaining mustard mixture in a small pan over high heat.

3 To serve, place spinach on a platter, top with chicken and pineapple, and drizzle with mustard mixture. Sprinkle with macadamias and season to taste with salt and pepper.

makes 4 servings

per serving: 341 calories, 31 g protein, 36 g carbohydrates, 10 g fat, 66 mg cholesterol, 649 mg sodium

chicken with two-tone pears

preparation time: about 30 minutes

Cooking Sauce (recipe follows)

3 tablespoons salad oil

2 cloves garlic, minced or pressed

2 whole chicken breasts (about 1 lb. *each*), skinned, boned, and cut into bite-size pieces

2 stalks celery, thinly sliced

3 green onions (including tops), cut into 2-inch lengths

1 can (about 8 oz.) sliced bamboo shoots, drained

¼ pound Chinese pea pods (also called snow or sugar peas) or sugar snap peas, ends and strings remove or 1 package (6 oz.) frozen Chinese pea pods, thawed and drained

1 *each* small red and yellow pear, quartered, cored, and cut into ½-inch-thick slices

Salt

½ cup salted roasted cashews

1 Prepare Cooking Sauce and set aside.

2 Place a wok over high heat; when wok is hot, add 1 tablespoon of the oil. When oil is hot, add garlic and half the chicken. Stir-fry until chicken is no longer pink in center; cut to test (about 3 minutes). Remove from wok and set aside. Repeat to cook remaining chicken, adding 1 tablespoon more oil.

3 Pour remaining 1 tablespoon oil into wok. When oil is hot, add celery, onions, and bamboo shoots; stir-fry for about 1 minute. Add pea pods and stir-fry for 3 minutes (30 seconds if using frozen pea pods), adding a few drops of water if wok appears dry. Add pears and chicken; stir Cooking Sauce and add. Stir until sauce boils and thickens. Season to taste with salt; garnish with cashews.

COOKING SAUCE

Stir together 4 teaspoons cornstarch, 1 teaspoon sugar, 2 teaspoons minced fresh ginger, 2 tablespoons each soy sauce and dry sherry, and ¾ cup regular-strength chicken broth.

makes 6 servings

per serving: 297 calories, 27 g protein, 17g carbohydrates, 14 g total fat, 57 mg cholesterol, 616 mg sodium

chicken breasts calvados

preparation time: about 45 minutes

1 large Golden Delicious apple peeled, cored, and thinly sliced

¼ cup apple brandy, brandy, or apple juice

¼ teaspoon ground nutmeg

2 skinless, boneless chicken breast halves (about 6 oz. *each*)

2 slices Havarti cheese

Chopped parsley

1 Divide apple slices between 2 shallow oven-proof 1½- to 2-cup ramekins. Pour 2 tablespoons of the brandy into each ramekin, then sprinkle ⅛ teaspoon of the nutmeg evenly over apples. Cover ramekins tightly with foil and bake in a 400° oven until apples are tender when pierced (about 20 minutes).

2 Rinse chicken and pat dry. Place one piece in each ramekin; baste with cooking juices, then sprinkle evenly with remaining ⅛ teaspoon nutmeg. Bake, uncovered, until meat in thickest part is no longer pink; cut to test (about 12 minutes).

3 Top each chicken piece with a cheese slice. Broil 6 inches below heat until cheese is bubbly (about 2 minutes). Sprinkle with parsley.

makes 2 servings

per serving: 413 calories, 46 g protein, 15 g carbohydrates, 10 g total fat, 128 mg cholesterol, 324 mg sodium

coq au vin sauté

preparation time: about 40 minutes

1 tablespoon salad oil

⅓ pound lean boneless pork (such as shoulder or butt), trimmed of excess fat and cut into ½-inch cubes

2 whole chicken breasts (about 1 lb. *each*), skinned, boned, and cut into ½- by 2-inch strips

1 large onion, finely chopped

½ pound small mushrooms, thinly sliced

1 can (14½ oz.) regular-strength chicken broth

1 cup dry red wine

2 tablespoons Dijon mustard

1 teaspoon *each* cornstarch and water, stirred together

2 tablespoons chopped parsley

1 Place a wok over medium-high heat; when wok is hot, add oil. When oil is hot, add pork and stir-fry until well browned (about 7 minutes). Lift out meat and set aside; leave drippings in wok.

2 Add half the chicken to wok. Stir-fry until meat is no longer pink in center; cut to test (3 to 4 minutes). Remove from wok and set aside. Repeat to cook remaining chicken.

3 Increase heat to high. Add onion and mushrooms; stir-fry until onion is soft (about 3 minutes). Remove vegetables from wok and set aside. Pour broth into wok, bring to a boil, and boil until reduced to 1 cup. Stir in wine and mustard and bring to a boil. Add pork, reduce heat, and simmer for 5 minutes.

4 Return chicken and vegetables to wok along with cornstarch-water mixture. Bring to a boil, stirring until slightly thickened. Sprinkle with parsley.

makes about 4 servings

per serving: 314 calories, 44 g protein, 9 g carbohydrates, 11 g total fat, 111 mg cholesterol, 806 mg sodium

chicken in tomato sauce

preparation time: about 45 minutes

1 frying chicken (3 to 3½ lbs.), cut up

2 tablespoons salad oil

Salt and pepper

2 tablespoons brandy

1 small onion, finely chopped

¼ pound mushrooms, sliced

1 fresh rosemary sprig (2 to 3 inches long) or 1 teaspoon dry rosemary

1 tablespoon all-purpose flour

½ cup dry white wine

1 can (about 14 oz.) pear-shaped tomatoes

Fresh rosemary sprigs (optional)

1 Pull off and discard all visible fat from chicken pieces, then rinse chicken and pat dry. With a heavy knife or cleaver, cut each chicken piece through bones into 2-inch lengths.

2 Place a wok over medium-high heat; when wok is hot, add oil. When oil is hot, add thickest dark-meat pieces of chicken and cook, turning, until browned on both sides (about 5 minutes). Add remaining chicken. Continue to cook, turning, until pieces are well browned on both sides and meat near thighbone is no longer pink, cut to test (about 15 more minutes). Season to taste with salt and pepper.

3 Add brandy; when liquid bubbles, carefully ignite (not beneath an exhaust fan or near flammable items), then shake wok until flames die down. Lift out chicken pieces. Spoon off and discard all but about 1 tablespoon of the drippings.

4 Add onion, mushrooms, and 1 rosemary sprig (or 1 teaspoon dry rosemary) to drippings in wok; stir-fry until onion is soft (about 4 minutes). Sprinkle in flour and stir until golden. Blend in wine and bring to a boil. Add tomatoes (break up with a spoon) and their liquid; bring to a simmer. Return chicken to wok and stir gently just until heated through. Garnish with rosemary, if desired.

makes 4 servings

per serving: 518 calories, 50 g protein, 8 g carbohydrates, 31 g total fat, 154 mg cholesterol, 308 mg sodium

turkey scaloppine alla pizzaiola

preparation time: about 40 minutes

Tomato-Caper Sauce (recipe follows)

1¼ pounds boneless turkey breast, cut into ½-inch-thick slices

All-purpose flour

1 egg beaten with 1 tablespoon water

2 tablespoons butter or margarine

1 tablespoon olive oil

¼ cup grated Parmesan cheese

Chopped parsley

1 Prepare Tomato-Caper Sauce and keep warm over lowest heat (or set aside, then reheat).

2 Rinse turkey and pat dry; then place slices between sheets of plastic wrap and pound with a flat-surfaced mallet until about ¼ inch thick. Dust with flour; dip into egg mixture to coat lightly.

3 Melt 1 tablespoon of the butter in oil in a wide frying pan over medium-high heat. Add turkey, a portion at a time (do not crowd pan); cook, turning once, until golden brown on both sides, adding remaining 1 tablespoon butter as needed. As turkey is cooked, transfer to a warm shallow platter, overlapping pieces slightly; keep warm.

4 To serve, sprinkle turkey with cheese, then top with hot Tomato-Caper Sauce and garnish with parsley.

TOMATO-CAPER SAUCE

Heat 1 tablespoon olive oil in a wide frying pan over medium-high heat. Add 3 small pear-shaped tomatoes, seeded and finely chopped; ½ teaspoon Italian herb seasoning or ⅛ teaspoon *each* dry basil, dry oregano, dry thyme, and dry marjoram; 1 clove garlic, minced or pressed; 1 tablespoon tomato paste; ½ cup dry white wine; and 2 teaspoons drained capers. Boil, stirring often, until tomatoes are soft (6 to 8 minutes).

makes 4 servings

per serving: 346 calories, 38 g protein, 7 g carbohydrates, 18 g total fat, 161 mg cholesterol, 341 mg sodium

raspberry-glazed turkey tenderloins

preparation time: about 25 minutes

4 turkey breast tenderloins (about 2 ¼ lbs. *total*)

½ cup seedless raspberry jam

6 tablespoons raspberry vinegar

¼ cup Dijon mustard

1 teaspoon grated orange peel

½ teaspoon dry thyme

1 Rinse turkey and pat dry; set aside. In a 2- to 3-quart pan, whisk together jam, vinegar, mustard, orange peel, and thyme. Bring to a boil over high heat and boil, stirring, until reduced by about a fourth (2 to 3 minutes). Reserve about ½ cup of the glaze and keep warm; coat turkey with some of the remaining glaze.

2 Set turkey on rack of a broiler pan. Broil about 4 inches below heat, turning and basting once with remaining glaze, until meat is no longer pink in center; cut to test (8 to 10 minutes). Slice crosswise and arrange on warm plates. Offer with reserved ½ cup glaze.

makes 4 to 6 servings

per serving: 337 calories, 48 g protein, 25 g carbohydrates, 4 g total fat, 127 mg cholesterol, 501 mg sodium

hazelnut chicken

preparation time: about 30 minutes

½ cup hazelnuts

2 tablespoons fine dry bread crumbs

1 egg white

2 tablespoons Dijon mustard

2 whole chicken breasts (about 1 lb. *each*),
skinned, boned, and split

Ground white pepper

All-purpose flour

1 tablespoon butter or margarine

1 tablespoon salad oil

2 tablespoons dry white wine

½ cup whipping cream

Watercress sprigs

1 Spread hazelnuts in a shallow baking pan and toast in a 350° oven until skins begin to split (8 to 10 minutes). Pour nuts onto a clean towel; rub nuts with towel to remove most of skins. Let cool slightly, then whirl in a blender or food processor until finely ground. Pour into a shallow dish, mix in crumbs, and set aside. In another shallow bowl, beat egg white with 1 tablespoon of the mustard; set aside.

2 Rinse chicken, pat dry, sprinkle lightly with white pepper, and dust with flour. Dip chicken in egg white mixture to coat lightly; then coat with hazelnut mixture. Melt butter in oil in a wide frying pan over medium heat. Add chicken and cook, turning once, until browned on both sides and no longer pink in thickest part; cut to test (10 to 12 minutes). Remove chicken from pan and arrange in a warm serving dish; keep warm.

3 Add wine, cream, and remaining 1 tablespoon mustard to drippings in pan. Boil over high heat, stirring constantly, until slightly thickened. Drizzle over chicken. Garnish with watercress.

makes 4 servings

per serving: 431 calories, 38 g protein, 8 g carbohydrates, 27 g total fat, 127 mg cholesterol, 398 mg sodium

chicken & apple sauté

preparation time: 40 to 45 minutes

2 whole chicken breasts (about 1 lb. *each*),
boned and split

¼ cup butter or margarine

2 large tart apples, peeled, cored, and cut into
¼-inch-thick slices

1 large onion, chopped

⅔ cup dry sherry or apple juice

⅓ cup whipping cream

1 Rinse chicken, pat dry, and set aside. Melt 2 tablespoons of the butter in a wide frying pan over medium heat. Add apples and cook, stirring often, just until tender when pierced (2 to 4 minutes). Lift out and keep warm.

2 Increase heat to medium-high and melt remaining 2 tablespoons butter in pan. Add chicken and cook, turning once, until lightly browned on both sides (7 to 8 minutes). Lift out and keep warm.

3 Add onion to pan and cook, stirring, until golden (about 7 minutes). Add sherry; boil for 1 minute. Return chicken to pan, skin sides up. Reduce heat, cover, and simmer until meat in thickest part is no longer pink; cut to test (about 5 minutes). Transfer to a warm platter; top with apples and keep warm. Add cream to pan and boil, stirring, until sauce is slightly thickened (2 to 3 minutes). Pour over chicken.

makes 4 servings

per serving: 396 calories, 35 g protein, 19 g carbohydrates, 20 g total fat, 139 mg cholesterol, 224 mg sodium

orange-herb chicken

preparation time: about 45 minutes

Orange-Herb Baste (recipe follows)

1 chicken (3 to 3¼ lbs.), cut up

Vegetable oil cooking spray

¼ cup regular-strength chicken broth

1 Prepare Orange-Herb Baste; set aside. Rinse chicken and pat dry.

2 Spray a shallow 12- by 15-inch baking pan with cooking spray. Set chicken breasts aside; place remaining chicken pieces, skin sides down, in pan and top evenly with about a third of the baste. Bake in a 400° oven for 15 minutes. Turn chicken over, add breasts to pan, and spoon remaining baste over chicken.

3 Return to oven and continue to bake until meat in thickest part of breasts is no longer pink; cut to test (about 20 more minutes). Transfer chicken to a warm platter and keep warm.

4 Pour broth into baking pan, stirring to scrape browned bits free; then pour into a 1 ½- to 2-quart pan. Bring to a boil over high heat, stirring; spoon over chicken.

ORANGE-HERB BASTE

Mix 1 can (6 oz.) frozen orange juice concentrate, thawed; ⅓ cup soy sauce; 1½ teaspoons minced fresh ginger or ½ teaspoon ground ginger; 1 clove garlic, minced or pressed; and 1 teaspoon *each* chopped fresh thyme, sage, marjoram, rosemary, and oregano (or ½ teaspoon *each* of the dry herbs).

makes 4 servings

per serving: 346 calories, 40 g protein, 23 carbohydrates, 10 g total fat, 113 mg cholesterol, 1,531 mg sodium

baked chicken quarters with port & grapes

preparation time: about 45 minutes

1 chicken (3 to 3¼ lbs.), cut into quarters

1 tablespoon butter or margarine, melted

Salt and ground white pepper

¾ cup regular-strength chicken broth

½ cup tawny port

1 tablespoon cornstarch, blended with 1 tablespoon water

1 tablespoon firmly packed brown sugar

⅛ teaspoon dry thyme

1½ cups seedless red grapes

1 Rinse chicken and pat dry. Brush skin sides with butter; sprinkle with salt and white pepper. Place chicken quarters, well apart and skin sides down, in a shallow baking pan. Bake in a 400° oven for 20 minutes. Turn over and continue to bake until skin is crisp and browned and meat near thighbone is no longer pink; cut to test (about 15 more minutes). Transfer chicken to a warm deep platter and keep warm.

2 Pour broth into baking pan, stirring to scrape browned bits free; then pour into a 2-quart pan. Add port, cornstarch mixture, sugar, and thyme. Boil over high heat, stirring constantly, until sauce is thickened and clear. Add grapes; stir just until heated through.

3 Pour half the port sauce over and around chicken. Pass remaining sauce at the table.

makes 4 servings

per serving: 329 calories, 38 g protein, 15 g carbohydrates, 13 g total fat, 121 mg cholesterol, 328 mg sodium

chutney chicken breasts

preparation time: 30 to 35 minutes

2 tablespoons rum

3 tablespoons butter or margarine, melted

About ⅓ cup seasoned fine dry bread crumbs

3 whole chicken breasts (about 1 lb. *each*), skinned, boned, and split

1 jar (about 9 oz.) chutney, chopped

2 tablespoons slivered blanched almonds

Hot cooked wild or brown rice

1 Combine rum and butter in a shallow pan. Spread crumbs in another shallow pan.

2 Rinse chicken and pat dry.

3 Then cup each piece, skinned side down, in the palm of your hand. Fill cavity with about 1 tablespoon of the chutney and 1 teaspoon of the almonds. Fold and roll chicken around filling to enclose. Dip each piece in butter mixture, then in crumbs, coating well on all sides. Place chicken rolls, seam sides down, in a 9- by 13-inch baking pan. Drizzle with any remaining butter mixture.

4 Bake in a 425° oven until meat in thickest part is no longer pink; cut to test (15 to 18 minutes). Spoon pan drippings over chicken. Serve with rice and remaining chutney.

makes 6 servings

per serving: 294 calories, 36 g protein, 16 g carbohydrates, 9 g total fat, 101 mg cholesterol, 364 mg sodium

thai chicken & basil stir-fry

preparation time: 40 to 45 minutes

6 dried shiitake mushrooms (*each* 2 to 3 inches in diameter)

Coconut Milk Cooking Sauce (recipe follows)

2 to 4 tablespoons salad oil

1 medium-size yellow onion, thinly sliced and separated into rings

3 cloves garlic, minced or pressed

2 tablespoons minced fresh ginger

2 whole chicken breasts (about 1 lb. *each*), skinned, boned, and cut into ½-inch-wide strips

5 green onions (including tops), cut into 1-inch pieces

1½ cups lightly packed slivered fresh basil leaves

Hot cooked rice

1 Soak mushrooms in warm water to cover until soft (10 to 15 minutes); drain well. Cut off and discard stems. Slice caps into ¼-inch slivers; set aside. Prepare Coconut Milk Cooking Sauce; set aside.

2 Heat 2 tablespoons of the oil in a wok or wide frying pan over high heat. Add yellow onion, garlic, and ginger; cook, stirring, until onion is lightly browned. With a slotted spoon, transfer onion mixture to a bowl; set aside. Add chicken to pan, a portion at a time (do not crowd pan); cook, stirring, until lightly browned (about 3 minutes), adding more oil as needed. As chicken is cooked, lift out and add to onion mixture.

3 Pour cooking sauce into pan; boil, stirring constantly, until reduced by about a third. Return onion mixture and chicken to pan. Add mushrooms, green onions, and basil; stir just until heated through. Serve over rice.

COCONUT MILK COOKING SAUCE

Mix ¾ cup canned or thawed frozen coconut milk, 3 tablespoons soy sauce, 3 tablespoons unseasoned rice vinegar or white wine vinegar, 1½ tablespoons fish sauce (nam pla) or soy sauce, and ½ to 1 teaspoon crushed red pepper flakes.

makes 4 servings

per serving: 410 calories, 39 g protein, 15 g carbohydrates, 22 g total fat, 86 mg cholesterol, 879 mg sodium

peanut chicken with rice

preparation time: about 45 minutes

1 cup long-grain white rice

1 package (about 10 oz.) frozen tiny peas, thawed and drained

3 tablespoons crunchy or smooth peanut butter

3 tablespoons plum jam or grape jelly

1½ teaspoons lemon juice

1½ teaspoons reduced-sodium soy sauce

1 teaspoon Asian sesame oil

2 teaspoons vegetable oil mixed with teaspoon ground ginger

1 pound skinless, boneless chicken breast, cut into pieces

2 tablespoons sliced green onion

Lemon wedges

1 In a 3- to 4-quart pan, bring 2 cups water to a boil over high heat; stir in rice. Reduce heat, cover, and simmer until liquid has been absorbed and rice is tender to bite (about 20 minutes). Stir peas into rice; remove from heat and keep warm. Fluff occasionally with a fork.

2 While rice is cooking, prepare sauce. In a small bowl, stir together peanut butter, jam, 2 tablespoons water, lemon juice, soy sauce, and sesame oil. Set aside.

3 Heat ginger oil in a wide nonstick frying pan or wok over medium-high heat. When oil is hot, add chicken and stir-fry until no longer pink in center; cut to test (4 to 6 minutes). Remove chicken from pan with a slotted spoon and keep warm. Discard drippings from pan and wipe pan clean (be careful; pan is hot).

4 Stir sauce well and pour into pan. Stir over medium heat just until smoothly blended and heated through. Add chicken and onion; remove pan from heat and stir to coat chicken and onion with sauce.

5 Spoon rice mixture onto a rimmed platter and top with chicken mixture. Offer lemon wedges to squeeze over stir-fry to taste.

makes 4 servings

per serving: 481 calories, 36 g protein, 58 g carbohydrates, 11 g total fat, 66 mg cholesterol, 312 mg sodium

turkey chorizo sausage

preparation time: about 40 minutes
cooling time: at least 8 hours

1 large onion, chopped

2 teaspoons *each* chili powder and dried oregano

1 teaspoon *each* cumin seeds and crushed red pepper flakes

1 cup low-sodium chicken broth

1 pound ground turkey or chicken breast

½ cup cider vinegar

1 In a wide frying pan, combine onion, chili powder, oregano, cumin seeds, red pepper flakes, and broth. Bring to a boil over high heat; boil, stirring occasionally, until liquid has evaporated and browned bits stick to pan. Add 2 tablespoons water, stirring to scrape browned bits free; cook until mixture begins to brown again. Repeat this deglazing step, adding 2 tablespoons of water each time, until onion is a rich brown color.

2 Add 2 tablespoons more water, then crumble turkey into pan; cook, stirring, until browned bits stick to pan. Repeat deglazing step, adding vinegar in 2-tablespoon portions, until mixture is a rich brown color. If made ahead, let cool; then cover and refrigerate until next day.

makes about 3½ cups

per serving: 48 calories, 8 g protein, 2 g carbohydrates, 0.5 g total fat, 20 mg cholesterol, 92 mg sodium

chili chicken chunks

preparation time: about 50 minutes for chicken, 5 to 10 minutes for each dip

Dips (choices and recipes follow)

3 whole chicken breasts (about 1 lb. *each*), split; 3 pounds chicken thighs (10 to 12); or half of each

¾ cup all-purpose flour

¼ cup yellow cornmeal

2 teaspoons chili powder

½ teaspoon *each* paprika and salt

¼ teaspoon *each* ground cumin and dry oregano leaves

⅛ teaspoon pepper

¾ cup beer

Salad oil

1 Prepare dips of your choice; set aside.

2 Skin and bone chicken; then rinse, pat dry, and cut into 1½-inch chunks. Set aside. In a bowl, mix flour, cornmeal, chili powder, paprika, salt, cumin, oregano, and pepper. Add beer and stir until batter is smooth. Add chicken pieces to batter; if making a combination batch, keep light and dark meat separate and add an equal amount of batter to each. Stir chicken to coat evenly.

3 Set a wok in a ring stand. Pour oil into wok to a depth of 1½ inches and heat to 350° on a deep frying thermometer. Lift chicken from batter, 1 piece at a time, and add to oil; add as many pieces as will fit without crowding. Cook, turning occasionally, until chicken is richly browned on outside and no longer pink in center; cut to test (about 2 minutes for breast pieces, 3 minutes for thigh pieces). Adjust heat as needed to maintain oil temperature at 350°. Lift out cooked chicken with a slotted spoon, drain on paper towels, and keep warm until all chicken has been cooked. If made ahead, let cool, then cover and refrigerate until next day. To reheat, arrange on paper towels in a rimmed 10- by 15-inch baking pan; bake in a 350° oven until hot (about 15 minutes).

4 Mound chicken in a napkin-lined basket. To eat, pick up pieces and dunk into dips.

makes 8 to 10 appetizer servings, 4 or 5 entrée servings

DIPS

You'll need 1½ to 2 cups. Use 1 dip or, for variety, make up several half-recipes. (All 3 dips can be made ahead and refrigerated for up to 1 day; stir well before serving.) If you like, include purchased sauces, such as a barbecue sauce or seafood cocktail sauce.

GUACAMOLE DIP

Pit, peel, and mash 2 medium-size ripe avocados. Blend avocados with ¼ cup sour cream or plain yogurt, 2 tablespoons lime or lemon juice, 2 tablespoons chopped fresh cilantro, ½ teaspoon ground cumin, and 2 to 4 tablespoons canned diced green chiles. Season to taste with salt and liquid hot pepper seasoning.

DIJON DIP

Blend 1 cup mayonnaise or sour cream with 8 to 10 tablespoons Dijon mustard, 2 teaspoons lemon juice, and ¼ teaspoon pepper.

HORSERADISH DIP

Blend 1 cup mayonnaise or sour cream with 8 to 10 tablespoons prepared horseradish and 4 teaspoons lemon juice.

per entrée serving chicken: 394 calories, 44 g protein, 22 g carbohydrates, 14 g total fat, 102 mg cholesterol, 348 mg sodium

per tablespoon guacamole dip: 22 calories, .33 g protein, 1 g carbohydrate, 2 g total fat, .10 mg cholesterol, 8 mg sodium

per tablespoon dijon dip: 73 calories, .10 g protein, 1 g carbohydrate, 8 g total fat, 5 mg cholesterol, 219 mg sodium

per tablespoon horseradish dip: 68 calories, .17 g protein, .83 g carbohydrate, 7 g total fat, 5 mg cholesterol, 58 mg sodium

raspberry-glazed turkey sauté

preparation time: about 35 minutes

3 green onions

⅓ cup seedless red raspberry jam or jelly

3 tablespoons raspberry or red wine vinegar

1 tablespoon Dijon mustard

½ teaspoon grated orange peel

**¾ teaspoon chopped fresh tarragon
or ¼ teaspoon dried tarragon**

**8 ounces dried eggless spinach fettuccine
or plain fettuccine**

1 teaspoon olive oil or vegetable oil

**2 turkey breast tenderloins (about 1 lb. *total*),
cut into ¼- by 2-inch strips**

About 1 cup fresh raspberries

Tarragon sprigs

BUYING AND STORING POULTRY Fresh poultry should never be left at room temperature for long. If you buy your chicken and turkey at a supermarket, make it one of the last items you pick up; then get it home and into the refrigerator as quickly as possible. Cook fresh poultry within 3 days of purchase. If you can't use it that soon, enclose it securely in heavy-duty foil, freezer paper, or plastic bags, then freeze for up to 6 months.

1 Trim and discard ends of onions. Cut onions into 2-inch lengths; then cut each piece lengthwise into slivers. Set aside. In a small bowl, stir together jam, vinegar, mustard, orange peel, and chopped tarragon; set aside.

2 In a 4- to 5-quart pan, cook fettuccine in about 8 cups boiling water until just tender to bite (8 to 10 minutes); or cook according to package directions.

3 Meanwhile, heat oil in a wide nonstick frying pan or wok over medium-high heat. When oil is hot, add turkey and 1 tablespoon water. Stir-fry just until turkey is no longer pink in center; cut to test (about 2 minutes). Add water, 1 tablespoon at a time, if pan appears dry. Remove turkey from pan with a slotted spoon and keep warm. Discard drippings from pan; wipe pan clean (be careful; pan is hot).

4 Add jam mixture to pan and bring to a boil over medium-high heat; then boil, stirring, just until jam is melted and sauce is smooth (about 1 minute). Remove from heat and stir in turkey and onions.

5 Drain pasta well and divide among 4 warm individual rimmed plates or shallow bowls; top with turkey mixture. Sprinkle each with raspberries and garnish with tarragon sprigs.

makes 4 servings

per serving: 435 calories, 36 g protein, 64 g carbohydrates, 3 g total fat, 70 mg cholesterol, 178 mg sodium

tahitian chicken breasts with bananas

preparation time: 45 minutes

3 to 4 tablespoons butter or margarine

2 whole chicken breasts (about 1 lb. *each*), skinned, boned, and split

8 small firm-ripe red or yellow bananas

1 tablespoon minced fresh ginger

¼ teaspoon crushed red pepper

1 medium-size onion, finely chopped

1 clove garlic, minced or pressed

1 medium-size tomato, finely chopped

⅓ cup finely chopped parsley

½ cup light rum (optional)

½ cup regular-strength chicken broth

1 cup whipping cream

Parsley sprigs

Lime wedges

1 In a wide nonstick frying pan, melt 2 tablespoons of the butter over high heat. Add chicken and cook, turning once, until browned on both sides; lift out and set aside, reserving drippings in pan.

2 Meanwhile, peel bananas. Chop 4 of them and set aside; cut remaining bananas in half lengthwise. Reduce heat to medium-high. Add banana halves to pan and cook, turning carefully, until browned, adding remaining butter as needed. Lift out bananas, reserving drippings in pan, and keep warm.

3 Add ginger and red pepper to pan; cook, stirring, for 1 minute. Add onion and garlic; cook, stirring often, for 5 minutes. Add tomato and chopped bananas; cook, stirring often, until bananas are soft (about 2 minutes). Stir in chopped parsley; transfer mixture to a bowl and keep warm.

4 Wipe pan clean. Pour in rum, if desired, broth, and cream; bring to a boil over high heat. Add chicken and any juices; reduce heat, cover, and simmer until meat in thickest part is no longer pink when slashed (6 to 7 minutes). Lift out chicken, reserving liquid in pan, and keep warm. Boil liquid over high heat, stirring occasionally, until reduced to ½ cup (about 5 minutes).

5 Arrange a chicken breast half and 2 banana halves on each of 4 plates. Spoon sauce over chicken; mound banana relish alongside. Garnish with parsley sprigs and lime.

makes 4 servings

per serving: 584 calories, 29 g protein, 48 g carbohydrates, 32 g total fat, 161 mg cholesterol, 341 mg sodium

lemon-oregano chicken

preparation time: about 45 minutes

½ cup lemon juice

2 tablespoons olive oil

1 tablespoon dried oregano

2 cloves garlic, pressed or minced

¼ teaspoon pepper

4 whole chicken legs (thighs with drumsticks; 2 ⅓ lbs. *total*)

Salt

1 In a large plastic food bag (or bowl), combine lemon juice, oil, oregano, garlic, and pepper.

2 Trim and discard excess fat from chicken legs. Rinse chicken and place in bag (or bowl). Seal and turn bag to mix chicken with marinade (or mix in bowl and cover airtight). Let stand 10 to 20 minutes, turning occasionally. If making ahead, chill chicken in marinade up to 1 day.

3 Lift chicken from marinade and place pieces slightly apart on a rack in a 10- by 15-inch broiler pan; reserve marinade.

4 Broil about 6 inches from heat, turning as needed to brown evenly, until meat is no longer pink at bone (cut to test), 25 to 30 minutes total; up until the last 10 minutes, baste occasionally with the reserved marinade. Add salt to taste.

makes 4 servings

per serving: 339 calories, 34 g protein, 1.6 g carbohydrates, 21 g total fat, 120 mg cholesterol, 117 mg sodium

lemon basil chicken

preparation time: about 25 minutes

½ cup butter or margarine

2 whole chicken breasts (about 1 lb. *each*), skinned, boned, and split

1 cup regular-strength chicken broth

2 teaspoons grated lemon peel

2 tablespoons lemon juice

3 tablespoons chopped fresh basil leaves or 1 tablespoon dry basil

Fresh basil leaves (optional)

1 In a wide frying pan, melt 2 tablespoons of the butter over medium-high heat. Add chicken and cook, turning once, until lightly browned (about 4 minutes total). Add broth, lemon peel, and lemon juice. Reduce heat, cover, and simmer until chicken is no longer pink in center when cut (about 5 more minutes). Transfer to a warm serving platter; keep warm.

2 Increase heat to high and boil pan juices until reduced by half (2 to 3 minutes). Reduce heat to medium; pour in any accumulated juices from chicken. Add remaining butter and cook, stirring, until sauce coats back of a spoon.

3 Stir in chopped basil. Pour sauce around chicken and garnish with basil leaves, if desired.

makes 4 servings

per serving: 379 calories, 35 g protein, 2 g carbohydrates, 25 g total fat, 148 mg cholesterol, 583 mg sodium

honey-dijon barbecued chicken

preparation time: about 40 minutes

12 chicken drumsticks (2½ to 3 lbs. *total*)

⅓ cup honey

2 tablespoons Dijon mustard

1 teaspoon grated fresh ginger

1 clove garlic, peeled and pressed or minced

1 teaspoon Worcestershire

Salt and pepper

1 If using charcoal, ignite 60 briquets on the firegrate of a barbecue with a lid. When briquets are dotted with gray ash, in 15 to 20 minutes, push equal amounts to opposite sides of firegrate. Set a drip pan on firegrate between mounds. If using a gas barbecue, turn all burners to high and close lid for 10 minutes Adjust burners for indirect cooking (heat on opposite sides of grill, not down center); keep heat on high.

2 Rinse chicken and pat dry. Set chicken on grill, not directly over heat. Cover (open vents for charcoal) and cook 20 minutes.

3 Meanwhile, in a small bowl, mix honey, mustard, ginger, garlic, and Worcestershire. Brush drumsticks generously with honey mixture. Cover and cook another 5 minutes.

4 Turn drumsticks; baste with honey mixture. Cover and cook until meat is no longer pink at bone in thickest part (cut to test), about 5 minutes longer. Transfer to a platter. Add salt and pepper to taste.

makes 6 servings

per serving: 296 calories, 29 g protein, 16 g carbohydrates, 12 g total fat, 98 mg cholesterol, 227 mg sodium

sesame chicken with stir-fry vegetables

preparation time: about 35 minutes

4 chicken breast halves (about 2 lbs. *total*), skinned and boned

1 teaspoon sesame seeds vegetable oil cooking spray

4 teaspoons rice vinegar

4 teaspoons reduced-sodium soy sauce

1½ teaspoons Asian sesame oil

1 tablespoon grated fresh ginger

2 cloves garlic, minced or pressed

½ teaspoon sugar

1 tablespoon vegetable oil

8 ounces mushrooms, sliced

4 cups thinly sliced red cabbage

4 ounces Chinese pea pods (also called snow peas), ends and strings removed

2 cups hot cooked rice

1 Rinse chicken, pat dry, and sprinkle with sesame seeds. Spray a ridged cooktop grill pan with cooking spray. Place over medium heat and preheat until a drop of water dances on surface. Then place chicken on grill and cook, turning once, until well browned on outside and no longer pink in thickest part; cut to test (12 to 15 minutes).

2 Meanwhile, in a small bowl, stir together vinegar, soy sauce, sesame oil, ginger, garlic, and sugar; set aside. Then heat vegetable oil in a wide non-stick frying pan or wok over medium-high heat.

3 Add mushrooms and cook, stirring often, for about 3 minutes. Add cabbage and cook, stirring often, until it begins to soften (about 2 minutes). Add pea pods and cook, stirring, just until they turn bright green (1 to 2 minutes). Add vinegar mixture and stir for 1 more minute.

4 Divide vegetables among 4 warm dinner plates. Cut each chicken piece diagonally across the grain into ½-inch-wide strips. Arrange chicken over vegetables; serve with rice.

makes 4 servings

per serving: 400 calories, 40 g protein, 40 g carbohydrates, 8 g total fat, 86 mg cholesterol, 310 mg sodium

turkey & mushroom burgers

preparation time: about 25 minutes

1 egg white

¼ cup dry white wine

⅓ cup soft French bread crumbs

¼ teaspoon salt

⅛ teaspoon pepper

¼ cup finely chopped shallots

1 pound lean ground turkey breast

4 ounces mushrooms, finely chopped

Olive oil cooking spray

6 onion hamburger rolls, split and warmed

1 In a medium-size bowl, beat egg white and wine until blended. Stir in bread crumbs, salt, pepper, and shallots; then lightly mix in turkey and mushrooms. Shape turkey mixture into 6 patties, each about ½ inch thick.

2 Spray a wide nonstick frying pan with cooking spray. Place over medium-high heat; add turkey patties. Cook, turning once, until patties are lightly browned on both sides and juices run clear when a knife is inserted in center (8 to 10 minutes). Serve on warm rolls.

makes 6 servings

per serving: 235 calories, 24 g protein, 25 g carbohydrates, 3 g total fat, 47 mg cholesterol, 394 mg sodium

turkey & green bean stir-fry

preparation time: about 30 minutes

Cooking Sauce (recipe follows)

1 egg white

2 tablespoons soy sauce

2 pounds turkey breast, skinned, boned, and cut into ¼- by 2-inch strips

¼ cup salad oil

½ pound green beans (ends removed), cut into 2-inch pieces

½ cup thinly sliced celery

½ cup thinly sliced onion, separated into rings

6 tablespoons water or dry sherry

1 or 2 cloves garlic, minced or pressed

1 Prepare Cooking Sauce; set aside.

2 In a bowl, beat together egg white and soy; add turkey and stir to coat. Set aside. Place a wok over high heat; when wok is hot, add 2 tablespoons of the oil. When oil is hot, add beans, celery, and onion; stir-fry for about 1 minute, then add water. Cover and cook, stirring occasionally, until beans are tender-crisp to bite (about 4 minutes).

3 Remove vegetables from wok, then add remaining 2 tablespoons oil. When oil is hot, add garlic and half the turkey. Stir-fry until meat is no longer pink in center; cut to test (about 3 minutes). Remove from wok. Repeat to cook remaining turkey; return all turkey to wok along with green bean mixture. Stir Cooking Sauce, pour into wok, and stir until sauce boils and thickens.

COOKING SAUCE

Mix 1 tablespoon each cornstarch and soy sauce, 2 tablespoons dry sherry, ½ teaspoon ground ginger, and ½ cup water.

makes 4 servings

per serving: 376 calories, 45 g protein, 10 g carbohydrates, 17 g total fat, 111 mg cholesterol, 922 mg sodium

chicken breasts with parmesan pesto

preparation time: about 30 minutes

6 skinless, boneless chicken breast halves (about 1½ lbs. *total*)

1 cup lightly packed fresh basil leaves

¾ cup grated Parmesan cheese

¼ cup olive oil

1 small clove garlic

1½ tablespoons butter or margarine

1½ tablespoons olive oil

About ⅓ cup all-purpose flour

Basil sprigs

1 Rinse chicken and pat dry. Place each breast half between 2 sheets of plastic wrap; pound with a flat-surfaced mallet to a thickness of about ¼ inch. Set aside.

2 In a blender or food processor, combine basil leaves, cheese, the ¼ cup oil, and garlic; whirl to form a thick paste. Then mound a sixth of the pesto in center of each pounded chicken breast half; roll chicken around pesto to enclose.

3 Melt butter in the 1½ tablespoons oil in a 12- to 14-inch frying pan over medium-high heat. Dip each chicken roll in flour and shake off excess; add chicken to pan. Cook, turning as needed, until meat is golden brown on all sides and no longer pink in center, and filling is hot; cut to test (about 10 minutes). Transfer to a serving dish and garnish with basil sprigs.

makes 6 servings

per serving: 338 calories, 32 g protein, 8 g carbohydrates, 20 g total fat, 81 mg cholesterol, 290 mg sodium

chicken with plum sauce

preparation time: about 50 minutes

Plum Sauce or Lemon Sauce (recipes follow)

1½ pounds chicken breasts or thighs, skinned, boned, and cut into about 1½-inch-square pieces

2 tablespoons soy sauce

1 tablespoon *each* cornstarch and water, stirred together

¼ teaspoon sesame oil

Dash of white pepper

Salad oil

1 cup all-purpose flour

¼ cup cornstarch

1½ teaspoons baking powder

1 cup water

1 Prepare sauce of your choice and set aside.

2 Pound chicken lightly with the back of a cleaver or heavy knife so pieces are of uniform thickness. In a bowl, stir together soy, cornstarch-water mixture, sesame oil, and white pepper. Add chicken and stir to coat, then stir in 1 tablespoon salad oil and let marinate for 15 minutes.

3 In another bowl, combine flour, the ¼ cup corn-starch, and baking powder. Add water and 1 tablespoon salad oil; blend until smooth. Let batter stand for 10 minutes.

4 Set a wok in a ring stand. Pour salad oil into wok to a depth of 1½ inches and heat to 350° on a deep-frying thermometer. Dip each piece of chicken in batter, then lower into oil; add as many pieces as will fit without crowding. Cook, turning occasionally, until crust is golden brown and meat is no longer pink in center; cut to test (about 2 minutes for breast pieces, about 4 minutes for thigh pieces). Adjust heat as needed to maintain oil temperature at 350°.

5 Lift out cooked chicken with a slotted spoon and drain on paper towels. Keep warm until all pieces have been cooked. Offer Plum Sauce or Lemon Sauce to spoon over chicken.

PLUM SAUCE

1 In a bowl, stir together ¾ cup water, 1 ½ teaspoons cornstarch, 2 teaspoons sugar, 1 teaspoon soy sauce, and ¼ cup canned plum sauce.

2 Heat 1 tablespoon salad oil in a small pan over medium-high heat. Add 2 tablespoons thinly sliced pickled red ginger and stir fry for 30 seconds. Pour in plum sauce mixture and cook, stirring, until sauce boils and thickens slightly (about 2 minutes). Let cool at room temperature before serving.

LEMON SAUCE

1 Cut 1 large thin-skinned lemon into thin slices; discard end pieces and any seeds. Heat 1 tablespoon salad oil in a small pan over medium-high heat. Add lemon slices and stir-fry for 30 seconds. Add 1 cup regular-strength chicken broth, and 3 tablespoons each sugar and lemon juice. Bring to a boil, then reduce heat and simmer for 2 minutes. Blend 1 tablespoon cornstarch with 1 tablespoon water. Pour into sauce and cook, stirring, until sauce boils and thickens slightly. Season to taste with salt.

2 Reheat sauce and pour over chicken just before serving.

makes 3 or 4 servings

per serving: 427 calories, 20 g protein, 50 g carbohydrates, 17 g total fat, 41 mg cholesterol, 703 mg sodium

chicken cacciatore presto

preparation time: 40 minutes

1 frying chicken (about 3 ½ lbs.), cut up

2 tablespoons olive oil or salad oil

¼ teaspoon salt

Pepper

2 tablespoons brandy

1 small onion, finely chopped

¼ pound mushrooms, sliced

1 fresh rosemary sprig (2 to 3 inches long) or 1 teaspoon dry rosemary

1 tablespoon all-purpose flour

½ cup dry white wine

1 can (about 16 oz.) pear-shaped tomatoes

1 Remove giblets from chicken and reserve for other uses. Pull off and discard all visible fat from chicken. Rinse chicken pieces and pat dry. With a cleaver or heavy knife, cut through bones of each piece of chicken to make 2-inch pieces.

2 Pour oil into a wide nonstick frying pan; place over medium-high heat. When oil is hot, add thickest dark-meat pieces of chicken and cook, turning, until browned on both sides (about 5 minutes total). Add remaining chicken and cook, turning, until pieces are well browned on both sides and meat near thighbone is no longer pink when slashed (about 15 more minutes). Sprinkle with salt and pepper.

3 Add brandy; when liquid bubbles, set aflame (not beneath an exhaust fan or near flammable items), shaking pan until flame dies. Lift out chicken pieces. Spoon off and discard all but about 1 tablespoon of the drippings.

4 In pan drippings cook onion, mushrooms, and rosemary, stirring often, until onion begins to brown. Sprinkle in flour and stir until golden. Blend in wine and bring to a boil. Add tomatoes (break up with a spoon) and their liquid and bring to a simmer. Return chicken to pan and cook, stirring gently, just until heated through.

makes 6 servings

per serving: 131 calories, 35 g protein, 7 g carbohydrates, 14 g total fat, 152 mg cholesterol, 192 mg sodium

garlic chicken & grapes

preparation time: 55 minutes

Vegetable oil cooking spray

6 whole chicken legs, thighs attached (about 3 lbs. total)

3 tablespoons each Dijon mustard and soy sauce

2 tablespoons each honey and white wine vinegar

2 cloves garlic, minced or pressed

1 tablespoon sesame seeds

2 cups red or green seedless grapes (about ¾ lb.)

Watercress sprigs

1 Spray a 9- by 13-inch baking pan with cooking spray. Place chicken legs in pan, skin side down. Cover with foil and bake in a 400° oven for 25 minutes.

2 While chicken is baking, combine mustard, soy sauce, honey, vinegar, and garlic in a small bowl; stir until well combined. Uncover chicken and turn skin side up. Pour mustard mixture over chicken and sprinkle with sesame seeds.

3 Return to oven and bake, uncovered, until meat near thighbone is no longer pink when slashed (about 15 minutes). Sprinkle grapes around chicken and bake just until grapes are heated through (3 to 5 more minutes).

4 Arrange chicken and grapes on a serving platter and spoon sauce over. Garnish with watercress.

makes 6 servings

per serving: 267 calories, 30 g protein, 17 g carbohydrates, 17 g total fat, 156 mg cholesterol, 760 mg sodium

hot & sour chicken

preparation time: about 25 minutes

Cooking Sauce (recipe follows)

2 teaspoons *each* **cornstarch, dry sherry, and salad oil**

¼ teaspoon pepper

1½ to 1¾ pounds chicken breasts, skinned, bone and cut into ¾-inch cubes

2 to 3 tablespoons salad oil

1 tablespoon finely chopped garlic

2 teaspoons finely chopped fresh ginger

1 tablespoon fermented salted black beans, rinsed, drained, and patted dry

1 green bell pepper, seeded and cut into 1-inch squares

1 carrot, thinly sliced

1 can (about 8 oz.) sliced bamboo shoots, drained

1 Prepare Cooking Sauce and set aside. In a bowl, stir together cornstarch, sherry, the 2 teaspoons oil, and pepper. Add chicken and stir to coat.

2 Place a wok over high heat; when wok is hot, add 2 tablespoons of the oil. When oil is hot, add chicken mixture; stir-fry for 2 minutes. Add 1 tablespoon more oil, if needed; then add garlic, ginger, and black beans. Stir-fry until chicken is lightly browned (about 2 more minutes). Then add bell pepper, carrot, and bamboo shoots; stir-fry for 2 minutes. Stir sauce and add; stir until sauce boils and thickens.

COOKING SAUCE

Stir together 2 teaspoons cornstarch, ½ teaspoon crushed dried hot red chiles, 2 tablespoons soy sauce, 2 ½ tablespoons white wine vinegar, and ½ cup regular-strength chicken broth.

makes 4 servings

per serving: 302 calories, 32 g protein, 9 g carbohydrates, 15 g total fat, 75 mg cholesterol, 843 mg sodium

chili-glazed chicken with peas

preparation time: about 45 minutes

1 chicken (3 to 3½ lbs.), cut up

⅓ cup butter or margarine, melted

2 cloves garlic, minced or pressed

1 teaspoon chili powder

¼ teaspoon *each* **ground cumin and grated lime peel**

2 tablespoons lime juice

2 pounds peas in the pod

2 tablespoons water

1 Rinse chicken and pat dry. In a small pan, stir together butter, garlic, chili powder, cumin, lime peel, and lime juice. Brush generously over chicken. Arrange chicken, except breast pieces, skin side up on a lightly greased grill 4 to 6 inches above a solid bed of medium coals. Cook for 15 minutes, turning and basting frequently with butter mixture. Place breast pieces on grill. Continue to cook, turning and basting often, until meat near thighbone is no longer pink; cut to test (about 25 more minutes).

2 Meanwhile, rinse peas; then place in a cast-iron frying pan or Dutch oven and add water. Cover with lid or foil; place on grill next to chicken during last 15 minutes of cooking, stirring peas every 5 minutes. Let guests shell their own peas to eat alongside chicken.

makes 4 servings

per serving: 599 calories, 49 g protein, 14 g carbohydrates, 38 g fat, 184 mg cholesterol, 299 mg sodium

chicken breasts with papaya & chutney

preparation time: about 25 minutes

3 tablespoons salad oil

½ cup sliced almonds

3 whole chicken breasts (about 1 lb. *each*), skinned, boned, and split

1 large papaya

1½ tablespoons lime or lemon juice

½ cup Major Grey's chutney, finely chopped

½ cup regular-strength chicken broth

1 teaspoon cornstarch

½ teaspoon each paprika and ground ginger

2 tablespoons butter or margarine

White pepper

Hot cooked spinach

1 Place a wok over medium heat; when wok is hot, add 1 tablespoon of the oil. When oil is hot, add almonds and stir until golden (about 2 minutes). Remove from wok and set aside.

2 Rinse chicken and pat dry. Cut each breast half across the grain into ½-inch-wide strips; set aside.

3 Peel and halve papaya; remove seeds. Cut each papaya half lengthwise into quarters, then cut each piece in half crosswise. Place in a bowl, add lime juice, and stir until fruit is coated. In another bowl, stir together chutney, broth, cornstarch, paprika, and ginger.

4 Place wok over medium-high heat. When wok is hot, add 1 tablespoon each of the butter and oil. When butter is melted, add half the chicken and stir-fry until meat is no longer pink in center; cut to test (about 3 minutes). Remove from wok and set aside. Repeat to cook remaining chicken, adding remaining 1 tablespoon each butter and oil. Return all chicken to wok.

5 Stir chutney mixture and add to chicken. Bring to a boil and stir until thickened (about 2 minutes). Add papaya and stir gently just until fruit is glazed and heated through. Season to taste with white pepper.

6 To serve, spoon chicken mixture over spinach; sprinkle with almonds.

makes 6 servings

per serving: 388 calories, 36 g protein, 23 g carbohydrates, 17 g total fat, 96 mg cholesterol, 267 mg sodium

easy oven-fried chicken

preparation time: about 50 minutes

4 skinless, boneless chicken breast halves (about 1 lb. *total*)

2 tablespoons dry sherry

2 cloves garlic, minced or pressed

½ cup soft whole wheat bread crumbs

2 tablespoons cornmeal

½ teaspoon salt

1 teaspoon paprika

½ teaspoon each pepper, dry sage leaves, dry thyme leaves, and dry basil leaves

1 teaspoon salad oil

1 Rinse chicken and pat dry. In a shallow bowl, combine sherry and garlic. Add chicken, turn to coat, and let stand for about 20 minutes.

2 In a wide, shallow rimmed plate, combine crumbs, cornmeal, salt, paprika, pepper, sage, thyme, and basil. Dip each chicken piece in crumb mixture to coat.

3 Brush a shallow 10- by 15-inch baking pan with oil. Arrange chicken in pan. Bake, uncovered, in a 450° oven until meat in thickest part is no longer pink; cut to test (about 20 minutes). Serve hot or cold.

makes 4 servings

per serving: 175 calories, 27 g protein, 8 g carbohydrates, 3 g fat, 66 mg cholesterol, 382 mg sodium

chicken breasts au poivre

preparation time: about 20 minutes

2 whole chicken breasts (about 1 lb. *each*), skinned, boned, and split

1 teaspoon crushed black peppercorns

4 teaspoons crushed pink peppercorns

2 to 3 tablespoons butter or margarine

½ cup Madeira or dry sherry

½ cup whipping cream

1 teaspoon minced fresh rosemary or ¼ teaspoon dry rosemary

Rosemary sprigs (optional)

1 Rinse chicken and pat dry, then place each piece between sheets of plastic wrap and pound with a flat-surfaced mallet until about ¼ inch thick. Sprinkle each side of each piece with ⅛ teaspoon of the black peppercorns and ½ teaspoon of the pink peppercorns; lightly pound peppercorns into chicken.

2 Melt 2 tablespoons of the butter in a wide frying pan over high heat. Add chicken pieces, a portion at a time (do not crowd pan). Cook, turning once, until meat in thickest part is no longer pink; cut to test (about 1 minute). As chicken is cooked, transfer to a warm platter and keep warm; add more butter to pan as needed.

3 Pour Madeira into pan, stirring to scrape browned bits free. Add cream and minced rosemary; boil, stirring often, until reduced by half. Pour over chicken. Garnish with rosemary sprigs, if desired.

makes 4 servings

per serving: 334 calories, 35 g protein, 6 g carbohydrates, 18 g total fat, 138 mg cholesterol, 183 mg sodium

chicken & green chile enchiladas

preparation time: about 45 minutes

8 to 10 small flour tortillas (*each* about 6 inches in diameter)

1 tablespoon salad oil

1 medium-size onion, thinly sliced

½ teaspoon ground cumin

¼ teaspoon dry oregano

1 can (4 oz.) diced green chiles

½ cup whipping cream

3 cups diced cooked chicken

1 small tomato, seeded and chopped

2 cups shredded jack cheese

1 cup shredded Cheddar cheese

Sour cream (optional)

Sliced ripe olives (optional)

1 Stack tortillas, wrap in foil, and place in a 350° oven until heated through (about 15 minutes).

2 Meanwhile, heat oil in a wide frying pan over medium heat. Add onion, cumin, and oregano; cook, stirring often, until onion is soft (about 10 minutes). Stir in chiles and cream. Boil over high heat, stirring often, until thickened (about 2 minutes). Add chicken and tomato; remove from heat and stir in 1 cup of the jack cheese.

3 Spoon an equal amount of chicken filling on each tortilla; roll up tortillas and place, seam sides down, in a single layer in a lightly greased 8- by 12-inch baking dish. Sprinkle with Cheddar cheese and remaining 1 cup jack cheese. Bake in a 425° oven until cheese is melted and enchiladas are heated through (12 to 15 minutes). Garnish with sour cream and olives, if desired.

makes 4 servings

per serving: 892 calories, 56 g protein, 36 g carbohydrates, 59 g total fat, 206 mg cholesterol, 1,103 mg sodium

garlic chicken & potatoes

preparation time: 50 to 55 minutes

4 whole chicken legs (1½ to 2 lbs. *total*)

3 tablespoons olive oil or salad oil

8 small red thin-skinned potatoes (*each* 1½ to 2 inches in diameter), scrubbed

1½ teaspoons minced fresh rosemary or 1 teaspoon dry rosemary

¼ cup water

24 large cloves garlic, peeled and slightly crushed

Salt and pepper

Rosemary sprigs (optional)

1 Rinse chicken and pat dry. Heat oil in a wide frying pan over medium-high heat. Add chicken and potatoes; cook, turning potatoes occasionally and chicken once, until chicken pieces are browned on both sides (10 to 12 minutes).

2 Reduce heat to low and add minced rosemary and water to pan. Cover and cook for 15 minutes. Turn chicken again and add garlic. Cover and continue to cook, turning potatoes and garlic occasionally, until potatoes are tender throughout when pierced and meat near thighbone is no longer pink; cut to test (about 10 more minutes). Transfer chicken, potatoes, and garlic to a warm platter.

3 Stir pan drippings, scraping browned bits free; pour over chicken and vegetables. Season to taste with salt and pepper. Garnish with rosemary sprigs, if desired.

makes 4 servings

per serving: 463 calories, 30 g protein, 23 g carbohydrates, 28 g total fat, 121 mg cholesterol, 124 mg sodium

chicken legs in cassis

preparation time: 45 to 50 minutes

4 whole chicken legs (1½ to 2 lbs. *total*)

Salt, ground white pepper, and ground nutmeg

2 tablespoons butter or margarine

1 tablespoon salad oil

1 clove garlic, minced or pressed

2 tablespoons cassis vinegar or raspberry vinegar

2 teaspoons tomato paste

¼ cup dried currants

¾ cup regular-strength chicken broth

¼ cup *each* dry white wine and crème de cassis (black currant liqueur)

1 tablespoon all-purpose flour

1 Rinse chicken, pat dry, and sprinkle with salt, white pepper, and nutmeg. Melt 1 tablespoon of the butter in oil in a wide frying pan over medium-high heat. Add chicken and cook, turning once, until browned on both sides (10 to 12 minutes). Stir in garlic, vinegar, and tomato paste; sprinkle with currants. Pour in broth, wine, and crème de cassis. Bring to a boil. Reduce heat, cover, and simmer until meat near thighbone is no longer pink; cut to test (about 25 minutes).

2 Smoothly mix flour with remaining 1 tablespoon butter; set aside. Lift chicken from pan, reserving drippings; transfer chicken to an oven-proof platter or shallow casserole and keep warm in a low oven while completing sauce. Boil liquid in frying pan over high heat, stirring often, until reduced by about a third. Blend in butter-flour mixture a little at a time, stirring constantly with a whisk, until sauce is thickened and shiny. Pour over chicken.

makes 4 servings

per serving: 413 calories, 28 g protein, 14 g carbohydrates, 27 g total fat, 136 mg cholesterol, 383 mg sodium

broiled chicken & cheese mexicana

preparation time: about 30 minutes

6 boneless chicken thighs (about 1¼ lbs. *total*), skinned

2 tablespoons lime or lemon juice

1 tablespoon red wine vinegar

2 tablespoons olive oil or salad oil

1 clove garlic, minced or pressed

⅛ teaspoon *each* salt, ground cumin, and crushed red pepper flakes

3 cups lightly packed shredded iceberg lettuce

1 medium-size firm-ripe avocado

½ cup shredded jack cheese

½ cup shredded sharp Cheddar cheese

1 medium-size tomato, cut into wedges

Lime wedges (optional)

Fresh cilantro sprigs (optional)

1 Rinse chicken and pat dry, then place pieces between sheets of plastic wrap and pound with a flat-surfaced mallet until about ¼ inch thick. In a small bowl, mix lime juice, vinegar, oil, garlic, salt, cumin, and red pepper flakes; reserve 2 tablespoons of the mixture, then brush chicken all over with some of the remaining mixture.

2 Place chicken on rack of a broiler pan. Broil about 4 inches below heat, turning once and brushing with remaining lime juice mixture, until meat in thickest part is no longer pink; cut to test (8 to 10 minutes).

3 Meanwhile, spread lettuce on a platter. Pit, peel, and slice avocado; drizzle avocado and lettuce with reserved 2 tablespoons lime juice mixture. Sprinkle chicken with jack and Cheddar cheeses; return to oven and continue to broil until cheese is melted (about 2 more minutes). Arrange chicken, avocado, and tomato on lettuce. Garnish with lime wedges and cilantro, if desired.

makes 3 servings

per serving: 519 calories, 39 g protein, 10 g carbohydrates, 37 g total fat, 149 mg cholesterol, 445 mg sodium

kauai chicken

preparation time: 35 to 40 minutes

8 small chicken thighs (2 to 2½ lbs. *total*)

¼ cup *each* granulated sugar and firmly packed brown sugar

⅓ cup soy sauce

2 tablespoons hoisin sauce

1 clove garlic, minced or pressed

1 Rinse chicken pieces, pat dry, and arrange, skin sides down, slightly apart in a shallow rimmed baking pan or casserole. Stir together granulated sugar, brown sugar, soy sauce, hoisin sauce, and garlic. Spoon about half the mixture over chicken.

2 Bake in a 400° oven for 20 minutes. Turn chicken over and top with remaining sauce. Return to oven and continue to bake until meat near bone is no longer pink; cut to test (10 to 15 more minutes).

makes 4 servings

per serving: 450 calories, 35 g protein, 30 g carbohydrates, 21 g total fat, 123 mg cholesterol, 1,728 mg sodium

minced turkey in lettuce

preparation time: 25 to 30 minutes

Cooking Sauce (recipe follows)

¼ cup salad oil

2 large cloves garlic, minced or pressed

1 teaspoon grated fresh ginger

¼ to ½ teaspoon crushed red pepper flakes

1 pound ground turkey; or 1½ pounds chicken breasts, skinned, boned, and minced

1 can (about 8 oz.) bamboo shoots, drained and minced

1 can (about 8 oz.) water chestnuts, drained and minced

¼ pound mushrooms, minced

4 green onions (including tops), minced

½ cup frozen peas

Hoisin sauce (optional)

Butter lettuce or romaine leaves, rinsed and crisped

2 green onions (green part only), cut into 1½-inch lengths

1 Prepare Cooking Sauce and set aside.

2 Heat 2 tablespoons of the oil in a wok or wide frying pan over high heat. Add garlic, ginger, and red pepper flakes and stir once. Add turkey and cook, stirring to break up large chunks, until no longer pink (about 3 minutes); remove from pan and set aside.

3 Heat remaining 2 tablespoons oil in pan. Add bamboo shoots, water chestnuts, mushrooms, and minced onions; cook, stirring, for 2 minutes. Return turkey to pan, then add peas. Stir Cooking Sauce, pour into pan, and stir until sauce boils and thickens. Serve immediately.

4 To eat, spread a little hoisin sauce (if used) on a lettuce leaf. Place a piece of green onion on top and spoon in some of the turkey mixture, then wrap up and eat out of hand.

COOKING SAUCE

Mix 2 teaspoons cornstarch, 1 tablespoon dry sherry, 2 tablespoons *each* soy sauce and water, and ½ teaspoon sugar.

makes 4 to 6 servings

per serving: 291 calories, 19 g protein, 13 g carbohydrates, 18 g total fat, 66 mg cholesterol, 521 mg sodium

game hens with mustard crust

preparation time: about 45 minutes

¼ cup butter or margarine

¼ cup coarse-grained or Dijon mustard

1½ teaspoons minced fresh rosemary or 1 teaspoon dry rosemary

2 cloves garlic, minced or pressed

4 Cornish game hens (1¼ to 1½ lbs. *each*), thawed if frozen and split lengthwise

Rosemary sprigs (optional)

1 Melt butter in a small pan; mix in mustard, minced rosemary, and garlic. Set aside.

2 Rinse hen halves, pat dry, and coat all over with mustard mixture. Set slightly apart, skin sides up, in a 9- by 13-inch baking pan.

3 Bake hen halves in a 450° oven until meat near thighbone is no longer pink; cut to test (about 35 minutes). Transfer to a warm platter and garnish with rosemary sprigs, if desired.

makes 4 servings

per serving: 721 calories, 68 g protein, 3 g carbohydrates, 47 g total fat, 251 mg cholesterol, 772 mg sodium

italian baked game hens & potatoes

preparation time: about 45 minutes

2 Cornish game hens (1¼ to 1½ lbs. *each*), thawed if frozen and split lengthwise

½ cup butter or margarine

¼ teaspoon *each* paprika, dry oregano, and dry thyme

2 large russet potatoes, scrubbed

Cherry tomatoes

1 Rinse hens; pat dry. Combine butter, paprika, oregano, and thyme in a small pan; stir over medium heat until butter is melted. Brush about 1 tablespoon of the herb butter over cut surfaces of hen halves; then place halves, skin sides up, slightly apart in a 9- by 13-inch baking pan.

2 Cut potatoes in half lengthwise; then cut each half lengthwise into 4 wedges. Brush cut surfaces of potatoes with remaining herb butter. Place potatoes, skin sides down, in a 9-inch-square baking pan.

3 Place pans side by side in a 450° oven. Bake until potatoes are tender when pierced and meat near thighbone is no longer pink; cut to test (about 35 minutes). Transfer hen halves to a warm platter; surround with potatoes and garnish with cherry-tomatoes.

makes 4 servings

per serving: 610 calories, 38 g protein, 21 g carbohydrates, 41 g total fat, 178 mg cholesterol, 351 mg sodium

FRENCH BAKED GAME HENS & POTATOES

Follow directions for Italian Baked Game Hens & Potatoes, but omit paprika, oregano, and thyme. Add 1 tablespoon finely minced onion to melted butter and cook, stirring, until onion is soft (about 10 minutes). Stir in a dash of liquid hot pepper seasoning and ¼ teaspoon each dry mustard, fines herbes, and garlic powder.

makes 4 servings

per serving: 610 calories, 38 g protein, 21 g carbohydrates, 41 g total fat, 178 mg cholesterol, 353 mg sodium

cinder chicken breasts

preparation time: 20 minutes

½ cup black sesame seeds

2 whole chicken breasts (about 1 lb. *each*), skinned, boned, and split

2 tablespoons butter or margarine

2 tablespoons soy sauce

Lemon wedges

1 Spread sesame seeds thickly in center of a large sheet of wax paper. Turn chicken pieces, one at a time, in seeds, patting seeds to coat solidly; shake off excess.

2 Place chicken in a single layer in a 9- by 13-inch baking dish. Bake, uncovered, in a 400° oven until meat in thickest part is no longer pink when slashed (about 15 minutes).

3 Meanwhile, in a small pan, melt butter over medium heat and stir in soy sauce. Garnish chicken with lemon and serve with soy sauce mixture.

makes 4 servings

per serving: 280 calories, 29 g protein, 5 g carbohydrates, 16 g total fat, 79 mg cholesterol, 646 mg sodium

brandied chicken breasts with pears

preparation time: 35 minutes

3 whole chicken breasts (about 1 lb. *each*), skinned, boned, and split

Salt and ground allspice

2 tablespoons butter or margarine

2 green onions (including tops), thinly sliced

1 teaspoon Dijon mustard

⅓ cup regular-strength chicken broth

2 medium-size pears, peeled, cored, and cut into thin wedges

¼ cup pear brandy or brandy

⅓ cup whipping cream

1 Season chicken with salt and allspice to taste. In a wide frying pan, melt butter over medium-high heat. Add chicken and cook, turning once, until golden brown on both sides. Add onions, mustard, and broth. Reduce heat, cover, and simmer for 10 minutes.

2 Add pear wedges, cover, and continue cooking just until pears are tender (6 to 8 minutes). Pour in brandy; set aflame (not beneath an exhaust fan or near flammable items), shaking pan until flames die. Lift out chicken and pears, reserving liquid in pan, and arrange on a warm serving dish; keep warm.

3 Add cream to pan. Boil over high heat, stirring often, until sauce is slightly thickened (2 to 3 minutes). Pour over chicken and pears.

makes 6 servings

per serving: 240 calories, 26 g protein, 12 g carbohydrates, 10 g total fat, 88 mg cholesterol, 195 mg sodium

fruited chicken stir-fry

preparation time: 30 minutes

Stir-fry Sauce (recipe follows)

2 whole chicken breasts (about 1 lb. *each*), skinned, boned, and split

1 large green bell pepper, seeded

1 medium-size onion

3 medium-size firm-ripe Santa Rosa-type plums

3 tablespoons salad oil

2 teaspoons minced fresh ginger

1 Prepare Stir-fry Sauce and set aside.

2 Cut chicken crosswise into ½-inch-wide strips. Cut green pepper and onion into 1-inch chunks. Slice plums into ½-inch-thick wedges, discarding pits. Heat 2 tablespoons of the oil in a wide frying pan or wok over high heat. Add chicken and ginger; stir-fry until meat is no longer pink when slashed (about 3 minutes). Lift out and set aside.

3 Heat remaining 1 tablespoon oil in pan. Add bell pepper and onion and stir-fry until tender-crisp (about 4 minutes); lift out and add to chicken. Add plums to pan; stir-fry until plums begin to soften (about 2 minutes). Stir sauce and add to pan; boil, stirring constantly, until thickened. Return chicken and vegetables to pan and cook, stirring gently, just until heated through.

STIR FRY SAUCE

Mix 1 cup canned peach nectar, ¼ cup lemon juice, 1 tablespoon cornstarch, 2 tablespoons soy sauce, and ½ teaspoon *each* dry mustard and crushed anise seeds.

makes 4 servings

per serving: 303 calories, 27 g protein, 22 g carbohydrates, 12 g total fat, 63 mg cholesterol, 594 mg sodium

chicken jambalaya

preparation time: about 1 1/2 hours

1 tablespoon salad oil

1/2 pound Canadian bacon, diced

1 1/2 pounds skinned and boned chicken breasts, cut into bite-size chunks

1 large onion, chopped

3 cloves garlic, minced or pressed

2 large green bell peppers, seeded and chopped

1 cup chopped celery

6 large tomatoes, chopped

1 large can (15 oz.) no-salt-added tomato sauce

2 bay leaves, crumbled

1 teaspoon dry thyme leaves

2 teaspoons ground white pepper

1 teaspoon ground red pepper (cayenne)

1/2 cup chopped parsley

1 1/2 cups long-grain white rice

3 cups low-sodium chicken broth

1 Heat oil in a 12- to 14-inch frying pan over medium heat. Add Canadian bacon and chicken; cook, stirring often, until browned on all sides (about 6 minutes). Transfer chicken to a 4- to 5-quart casserole.

2 Add onion, garlic, bell peppers, and celery to pan. Cook, stirring occasionally, until onion is soft (about 10 minutes). Add tomatoes, tomato sauce, bay leaves, thyme, white pepper, red pepper, and parsley; cook, stirring occasionally, until sauce boils. Boil gently, uncovered, for 5 minutes.

3 Pour sauce over chicken; stir in rice and broth. Cover and bake in a 375° oven until rice is tender to bite (about 45 minutes).

makes 6 servings

per serving: 471 calories, 42 g protein, 57 g carbohydrates, 8 g total fat, 85 mg cholesterol, 685 mg sodium

apricot-mustard chicken

preparation time: about 30 minutes

1 can (12 oz.) apricot nectar

3 tablespoons Dijon mustard

3 whole chicken breasts (about 1 lb. *each*), skinned, boned, and split

2 1/2 cups low-sodium chicken broth

10 ounces (about 1 3/4 cups) couscous

2 tablespoons minced fresh basil leaves

Basil sprigs and lime wedges (optional)

1 In a wide frying pan, combine apricot nectar and mustard. Bring to a boil over high heat. Arrange chicken breasts, skinned sides down, in pan. Reduce heat, cover, and simmer for 10 minutes. Turn chicken and continue cooking until meat in thickest part is no longer pink; cut to test (5 to 8 more minutes).

2 Meanwhile, bring chicken broth to a boil in a 2- to 3-quart pan over high heat; stir in couscous. Cover, remove from heat, and let stand until broth is completely absorbed (about 5 minutes).

3 With a fork, fluff couscous; transfer to a platter. Lift out chicken with a slotted spoon and arrange over couscous; keep warm.

4 Boil apricot mixture over high heat, stirring often, until reduced to 1 cup (about 5 minutes). Pour over chicken and sprinkle with minced basil. Garnish with basil sprigs and lime, if desired.

makes 6 servings

per serving: 380 calories, 41 g protein, 46 g carbohydrates, 3 g total fat, 86 mg cholesterol, 352 mg sodium

salsa chicken

preparation time: about 30 minutes

2 medium-size tomatoes, chopped and drained well

¼ cup thinly sliced green onions

¼ cup lime juice

1 small fresh jalapeño chile, seeded and finely chopped

1 tablespoon chopped cilantro

1 clove garlic, minced or pressed

About 8 cups finely shredded iceberg lettuce

2 large egg whites

½ cup yellow cornmeal

1 ½ teaspoons chili powder

½ teaspoon ground cumin

1 pound skinless, boneless chicken breast, cut into 1-inch pieces

2 teaspoons olive oil or vegetable oil

½ cup nonfat sour cream

Cilantro sprigs

1 To prepare tomato salsa, in a large bowl, combine tomatoes, onions, lime juice, jalapeño, chopped cilantro, and garlic; set aside. (At this point, you may cover and refrigerate for up to 3 hours.) Divide lettuce among 4 individual plates; cover and set aside.

2 In a shallow bowl, beat egg whites to blend; set aside. In a large bowl, combine cornmeal, chili powder, and cumin. Add chicken and turn to coat. Then lift chicken from bowl, shaking off excess coating. Dip chicken into egg whites, then coat again with remaining cornmeal mixture.

3 Heat oil in a wide nonstick frying pan or wok over medium-high heat. When oil is hot, add chicken and stir-fry gently until no longer pink in center; cut to test (5 to 7 minutes). Remove from pan and keep warm. Pour reserved salsa into pan; reduce heat to medium and cook, stirring, until salsa is heated through and slightly thickened (1 to 2 minutes).

4 Arrange chicken over lettuce; top with salsa and sour cream. Garnish with cilantro sprigs.

makes 4 servings

per serving: 284 calories, 34 g protein, 26 g carbohydrates, 5 g total fat, 66 mg cholesterol, 152 mg sodium

chicken with pumpkin seeds

preparation time: about 35 minutes

4 chicken breast halves (about 1 ¾ lbs. *total*), skinned and trimmed of fat

⅓ cup roasted pumpkin seeds

1 can (about 4 oz.) diced green chiles

½ cup shredded jack cheese

Lime wedges

1 Rinse chicken and pat dry; then place, skinned side up, in a 9- by 13-inch baking pan. In a small bowl, mix pumpkin seeds, chiles, and cheese; pat evenly onto chicken.

2 Bake chicken in a 450° oven until meat near bone is no longer pink; cut to test (20 to 25 minutes). Serve with lime wedges.

makes 4 servings

per serving: 226 calories, 35 g protein, 5 g carbohydrates, 7 g total fat, 90 mg cholesterol, 334 mg sodium

spicy chicken tortas

preparation time: about 35 minutes

TORTAS:

1 pound skinless, boneless chicken thighs

2 cups fat-free reduced-sodium chicken broth

¼ cup chili powder

¼ cup firmly packed brown sugar

2 teaspoons dried oregano

1 teaspoon anise seeds

About 1 tablespoon red wine vinegar, or to taste

2 tablespoons chopped cilantro

2 tablespoons thinly sliced green onion

4 French rolls

8 to 12 butter lettuce leaves, rinsed and crisped

CONDIMENTS:

avocado slices

asadero or string cheese

1 Rinse chicken and pat dry; set aside. In a 4- to 5-quart pan with a tight-fitting lid, combine 4 cups water, broth, chili powder, sugar, oregano, and anise seeds. Bring to a rolling boil over high heat. Remove pan from heat and immediately add chicken. Cover pan and let stand until meat in thickest part is no longer pink; cut to test (15 to 20 minutes; do not uncover until ready to test). If chicken is not done, return it to hot water, cover, and let steep for 2 to 3 more minutes.

2 Drain chicken, reserving 2 cups of the cooking liquid. Return reserved liquid to pan. Bring to a boil over high heat; boil until reduced to ½ cup, watching closely to prevent scorching.

3 Serve chicken and sauce warm or cold. To serve, stir vinegar, cilantro, and onion into sauce. Cut chicken diagonally across the grain into thin slices; set aside. Cut rolls in half lengthwise and moisten cut surfaces evenly with sauce. Fill rolls with chicken and lettuce. Offer additional sauce and condiments to add to taste.

makes 4 servings

per serving: 464 calories, 33 g protein, 68 g carbohydrates, 7 g total fat, 94 mg cholesterol, 1,819 mg sodium

greek chicken pockets

preparation time: about 30 minutes

Herb Dressing (recipe follows)

4 to 6 pita breads (*each* about 6 inches in diameter)

3 small firm-ripe tomatoes, thinly sliced

2 small green bell peppers, seeded and thinly sliced

3 cups shredded cooked chicken

¼ cup crumbled feta cheese

1 Prepare Herb Dressing.

2 Cut each pita bread in half; gently open halves and fill equally with tomatoes, bell peppers, chicken, and cheese. Then spoon dressing into each sandwich.

makes 4 to 6 servings

HERB DRESSING

In a small bowl, stir together 1 cup plain nonfat yogurt, ½ cup minced peeled cucumber, and 1 tablespoon each minced fresh dill and minced fresh mint (or 1 teaspoon each dry dill weed and dry mint).

per serving: 397 calories, 34 g protein, 44 g carbohydrates, 9 g total fat, 82 mg cholesterol, 512 mg sodium

stuffed chicken breasts with chutney

preparation time: about 50 minutes

1 tablespoon olive oil

2 cloves garlic, minced or pressed

1 large onion, chopped

2 1/4 cups chopped spinach leaves

4 whole chicken breasts, skinned, boned, and split

1 tablespoon balsamic vinegar

1/2 cup low-sodium chicken broth

1/4 cup chutney

1 Heat oil in a 12- to 14-inch frying pan over medium-high heat. Add garlic and onion and cook, stirring occasionally, until onion is soft (about 7 minutes). Add 2 cups of the spinach; let cool.

2 Rinse chicken; pat dry. Place each breast half between 2 sheets of plastic wrap. Pound with a flat-surfaced mallet to a thickness of about 1/4 inch.

3 In center of each breast half, mound an equal portion of the spinach mixture. Roll meat around filling to enclose; fasten with wooden picks. Place chicken rolls in pan used for spinach.

4 In a small bowl, mix vinegar, broth, and chutney. Pour over chicken. Bring to a simmer over medium heat. Cover and simmer until meat is no longer pink and filling is hot in center; cut to test (about 8 minutes). Remove chicken from pan; remove wooden picks and keep chicken warm.

5 Increase heat to high and bring chutney mixture to a boil. Cook, stirring occasionally, until reduced to 1/2 cup (about 5 minutes); then pour over chicken. Garnish with remaining 1/4 cup spinach.

makes 8 servings

per serving: 174 calories, 27 g protein, 8 g carbohydrates, 3 g total fat, 66 mg cholesterol, 107 mg sodium

sherried chicken with onion marmalade

preparation time: about 35 minutes
marinating time: at least 30 minutes

6 small boneless, skinless chicken breast halves (1 1/2 to 1 3/4 lbs. *total*)

3 tablespoons cream sherry

2 small red onions

1/2 cup dry red wine

1 tablespoon *each* red wine vinegar and honey

Italian or regular parsley sprigs

Salt and pepper

1 Rinse chicken, pat dry, and place in a heavy-duty plastic food-storage bag; add 2 tablespoons of the sherry. Seal bag and rotate to coat chicken with sherry Refrigerate for at least 30 minutes or up to 6 hours, turning bag over several times.

2 Thinly slice onions; wrap several slices airtight and refrigerate. In a wide frying pan, combine remaining onion slices, wine, vinegar, and honey. Cook over medium-high heat, stirring often, until liquid has evaporated. Remove from heat and stir in remaining 1 tablespoon sherry. Set aside.

3 Turn chicken and its marinade into a 9- by 13-inch baking pan; arrange chicken, skinned side up, in a single layer. Bake in a 450° oven until meat in thickest part is no longer pink; cut to test (12 to 15 minutes). With a slotted spoon, transfer chicken to a platter. Top with onion mixture. Garnish with reserved onion slices and parsley sprigs. Season to taste with salt and pepper.

makes 6 servings

per serving: 200 calories, 30 g protein, 9 g carbohydrates, 2 g total fat, 74 mg cholesterol, 91 mg sodium

chicken chimichangas

preparation time: about 15 minutes
cooking time: about 40 minutes

Shredded Chicken Filling (page 222)

About 1 1/2 cups salsa of your choice

5 cups shredded lettuce

1 1/2 cups shredded carrots

8 flour tortillas (7- to 9-inch diameter)

About 1/3 cup nonfat milk

1/2 cup shredded Cheddar cheese

Plain nonfat yogurt

1 Prepare Shredded Chicken Filling; set aside. In a small bowl, mix lettuce and carrots; set aside.

2 To assemble each chimichanga, brush both sides of a tortilla liberally with milk; let stand briefly to soften tortilla. Spoon an eighth of the filling down the center of tortilla; top with 1 tablespoon of the cheese. Lap ends of tortilla over filling; then fold sides to center to make a packet. Place chimichanga, seam side down, on a lightly oiled 12- by 15-inch baking sheet and brush with milk. Repeat to make 7 more chimichangas.

3 Bake in a 500° oven, brushing with milk after 5 minutes, until golden brown (8 to 10 minutes).

4 To serve, divide lettuce mixture among 8 plates; place 1 chimichanga on each plate. Add salsa and yogurt to taste.

makes 8 servings

per serving: 291 calories, 19 g protein, 37 g carbohydrates, 9 g total fat, 38 mg cholesterol, 338 mg sodium

oregano-rubbed turkey

preparation time: about 20 minutes
marinating time: at least 2 hours

1 tablespoon salt

1 1/2 teaspoons sugar

1 1/2 pounds thinly sliced turkey breast

1/4 cup sliced green onions

2 tablespoons finely chopped Italian or regular parsley

3 cloves garlic, minced

1 teaspoon chopped fresh oregano or 1/2 teaspoon dried oregano

1/2 teaspoon *each* coarsely ground pepper and grated lemon peel

2 teaspoons olive oil

Italian or regular parsley sprigs

Lemon wedges

1 In a large bowl, combine salt and sugar. Rinse turkey and pat dry; then add to bowl and turn to coat evenly with salt mixture. Cover and refrigerate for at least 2 hours or up to 3 hours. Rinse turkey well, drain, and pat dry.

2 In a small bowl, combine onions, chopped parsley, garlic, oregano, pepper, and lemon peel. Rub onion mixture evenly over both sides of each turkey slice.

3 Heat 1 teaspoon of the oil in a wide nonstick frying pan over medium-high heat. Add half the turkey and cook until golden on bottom (about 1 1/2 minutes). Then turn pieces over and continue to cook until no longer pink in center; cut to test (30 to 60 more seconds). Transfer cooked turkey to a platter, cover loosely with foil, and keep warm.

4 Immediately cook remaining turkey, using remaining 1 teaspoon oil; add water, 1 tablespoon at a time, if pan appears dry. Transfer turkey to platter and garnish with parsley sprigs. Serve at once. Season to taste with lemon.

makes 6 servings

per serving: 148 calories, 28 g protein, 2 g carbohydrates, 2 g total fat, 70 mg cholesterol, 1,155 mg sodium

chili & anise chicken tortas

preparation time: about 35 minutes

1 pound skinless, bone less chicken thighs

4 cups water

2 cups low-sodium chicken broth

1/4 cup chili powder

4 cup firmly packed brown sugar

2 teaspoons dried oregano

1 teaspoon anise seeds

About 1 tablespoon red wine vinegar, or to taste

2 tablespoons *each* chopped cilantro and thinly sliced green onion

4 French rolls (*each* about 6 inches long)

8 to 12 butter lettuce leaves, rinsed and crisped

CONDIMENTS:

Avocado slices and asadero or string cheese

1 Rinse chicken and pat dry; set aside. In a 4- to 5-quart pan with a tight-fitting lid, combine water, broth, chili powder, sugar, oregano, and anise seeds. Bring to a rolling boil over high heat. Remove pan from heat and immediately add chicken. Cover pan and let stand until meat in thickest part is no longer pink; cut to test (15 to 20 minutes; do not uncover until ready to test). If chicken is not done, return it to hot water, cover, and let steep for 2 to 3 more minutes.

2 Drain chicken, reserving 2 cups of the cooking liquid. Return reserved liquid to pan. Bring to a boil over high heat; boil until reduced to 1/2 cup, watching closely to prevent scorching.

3 Serve chicken and sauce warm or cold. To serve, stir vinegar, cilantro, and onion into sauce. Cut chicken across the grain into thin slanting slices; set aside. Cut rolls in half lengthwise and moisten cut surfaces evenly with sauce. Fill rolls with chicken and lettuce. Offer additional sauce and condiments to add to taste.

makes 4 servings

per serving: 464 calories, 33 g protein, 68 g carbohydrates, 7 g total fat, 94 mg cholesterol, 1,819 mg sodium

brunch paella

preparation time: about 55 minutes

1 pound turkey Italian sausages (casings removed), crumbled into 1/2-inch pieces

1 cup long-grain white rice

1 large onion (about 8 oz.), chopped

2 cloves garlic, minced or pressed

2 cups fat-free reduced sodium chicken broth

1 1/2 cups chopped tomatoes

1/4 teaspoon saffron threads

1 package (about 9 oz.) frozen artichoke hearts, thawed and drained

1/4 cup chopped parsley

Lemon wedges

1 In a wide nonstick frying pan or wok, stir-fry sausage over medium-high heat until browned (7 to 10 minutes). Remove sausage from pan with a slotted spoon; set aside. Pour off and discard all but 1 teaspoon fat from pan.

2 Add rice to pan; stir-fry until rice begins to torn opaque (about 3 minutes). Add onion, garlic, and 2 tablespoons water; stir-fry for 5 more minutes. Add more water, 1 tablespoon at a time, if pan appears dry.

3 Stir in broth, tomatoes, saffron, artichokes, and parsley; then return sausage to pan. Bring to a boil; reduce heat, cover, and simmer until liquid has been absorbed and rice is tender to bite (about 20 minutes). Serve with lemon wedges.

makes 4 to 6 servings

per serving: 195 calories, 7 g protein, 41 g carbohydrates, 0.7 g total fat, 0 mg cholesterol, 294 mg sodium

jalapeño chicken with mole poblano

preparation time: about 45 minutes

1 tablespoon sesame seeds

1 large onion, chopped

4 cloves garlic, minced or pressed

1 small very ripe banana, chopped

¼ cup chopped pitted prunes

2 tablespoons raisins

1 tablespoon creamy peanut butter

5 tablespoons unsweetened cocoa powder

3 tablespoons chili powder

2 teaspoons sugar

½ teaspoon ground cinnamon

⅛ teaspoon ground coriander

⅛ teaspoon ground cumin

⅛ teaspoon ground cloves

⅛ teaspoon anise seeds, crushed

2 cups fat-free reduced-sodium chicken broth

1 small can (about 6 oz.) tomato paste

8 skinless, boneless chicken breast halves
(about 6 oz. *each*)

1 Toast sesame seeds in a wide nonstick frying pan over medium heat until golden (about 4 minutes), stirring often. Transfer to a bowl; set aside.

2 To pan, add onion, garlic, banana, prunes, raisins, peanut butter, and 3 tablespoons water. Cook over medium heat, stirring often, until mixture is richly browned (10 to 15 minutes); if pan appears dry, add more water, 1 tablespoon at a time. Stir in cocoa, chili powder, sugar, cinnamon, coriander, cumin, cloves, anise seeds, and ¾ cup of the broth. Bring mixture to a boil over medium-high heat.

3 Transfer hot onion mixture to a food processor or blender and add tomato paste, 2 teaspoons of the anise seeds, and a little of the remaining broth. Whirl until smoothly puréed; then stir in remaining broth. Cover and keep warm. (At this point, you may let cool; then cover and refrigerate for up to 3 days; freeze for longer storage. Reheat before continuing.)

4 While onion mixture is browning, rinse chicken and pat dry. Place jelly in a bowl and stir to soften; add chicken in a lightly oiled 10- by 15-inch rimmed baking pan. Bake in a 450° oven until meat in thickest part is no longer pink; cut to test (12 to 15 minutes).

5 To serve, spoon some of the warm mole sauce onto dinner plates; top with chicken, then more mole sauce. Sprinkle with remaining 1 teaspoon sesame seeds. Season to taste with salt; serve with lime wedges to squeeze over chicken to taste.

makes 8 servings

per serving: 264 calories, 34 g protein, 23 g carbohydrates, 6 g total fat, 74 mg cholesterol, 322 mg sodium

MICROWAVE A WHOLE FRYING CHICKEN: Remove neck and giblets; reserve for other uses, if desired. Discard lumps of fat. Rinse chicken inside and out, and pat dry. Stuff, if desired and close stuffed cavities with string and wooden picks (not metallic skewers). Place, breast down, on a nonmetallic rack in a 7 by 11-inch microwave-proof baking dish. Cover with heavy-duty plastic wrap or wax paper. For a 3- to 3 ½-pound bird, microwave on HIGH for 6 to 7 minutes per pound, turning chicken over and rotating dish a quarter turn halfway through cooking.

saffron & honey chicken

preparation time: about 1 hour

2/3 **cup low-sodium chicken broth**

2 tablespoons *each* **lime juice and honey**

1/4 **teaspoon saffron threads**

1 teaspoon white Worcestershire

2 teaspoons curry powder

1/2 **teaspoon dry oregano**

1/4 **teaspoon paprika**

1/8 **teaspoon pepper**

2 teaspoons reduced-sodium soy sauce

2 tablespoons white rice flour blended with
1/4 cup cold water

6 *each* **chicken drumsticks and thighs (about**
3 lbs. *total***), skinned and trimmed of fat**

Chopped parsley

1 In a 1 1/2- to 2-quart pan, stir together broth, lime juice, honey, saffron, Worcestershire, curry powder, oregano, paprika, pepper, and soy sauce. Bring to a boil over high heat; then reduce heat and simmer, uncovered, stirring occasionally, until reduced to 1/2 cup (about 15 minutes). Stir in rice flour mixture; bring to a boil over high heat, stirring. Remove from heat.

2 Rinse chicken, pat dry, and arrange, skinned side up, in a 9- by 13-inch baking pan. Spoon sauce evenly over chicken. Cover and bake in a 375° oven until meat near bone is no longer pink; cut to test (about 35 minutes).

3 Transfer chicken to a platter; stir sauce to blend, then spoon over chicken. Sprinkle with parsley.

makes 6 servings

per serving: 198 calories, 27 g protein, 10 g carbohydrates, 5 g total fat, 104 mg cholesterol, 193 mg sodium

chicken and black bean bake

preparation time: about 35 minutes

1 package (about 7 oz.) or 1 2/3 **cups instant**
refried black bean mix

2 cups boiling water

1/3 **to** 1/2 **cup dry sherry or water**

4 boneless, skinless chicken breast halves (about
1 1/2 **lbs. total)**

8 cups shredded iceberg lettuce

1/2 **cup shredded jack cheese**

1 fresh red or green jalapeño chile, thinly sliced
crosswise (optional)

Cherry tomatoes

Reduced-fat sour cream

1 In a shallow 2- to 2 1/2-quart baking dish, combine refried bean mix, boiling water, and sherry (use the 1/2-cup amount if you prefer a saucelike consistency). Rinse chicken and pat dry; then arrange, skinned side up, atop beans. Bake in a 400° oven until meat in thickest part is no longer pink; cut to test (about 20 minutes). Stir any liquid that accumulates around chicken into beans.

2 Mound lettuce equally on 4 individual plates; top with beans and chicken. Sprinkle with cheese and chile (if used); garnish with cherry tomatoes. Offer sour cream to add to taste.

makes 4 servings

per serving: 469 calories, 54 g protein, 36 g carbohydrates, 8 g total fat, 114 mg cholesterol, 597 mg sodium

sake-steamed chicken

preparation time: about 30 minutes
marinating time: at least 30 minutes

1/2 **cup sake or unseasoned rice vinegar**

1/2 **teaspoon salt**

6 **boneless, skinless chicken breast halves (about 2** 1/4 **lbs.** *total***)**

1 **small head iceberg lettuce**

About 1/3 **cup reduced-sodium soy sauce**

1 **tablespoon prepared horseradish**

Lemon wedges

3 **cups hot cooked rice**

1/2 **cup thinly sliced green onions**

1 In a medium-size bowl, stir together sake and salt until salt is dissolved. Rinse chicken and pat dry; add to marinade and turn to coat. Cover and refrigerate for at least 30 minutes or up to 2 hours.

2 Lift chicken from bowl and drain briefly; discard marinade. Arrange chicken, with thickest parts toward outside, in a single layer in a 10- to 11-inch round heatproof nonmetal dish. Cover with wax paper or foil and set on a rack in a large pan above 1 inch of boiling water. Cover and steam, keeping water at a steady boil, until meat in thickest part is no longer pink; cut to test (about 12 minutes).

3 Meanwhile, place 1 or 2 large lettuce leaves on each of 6 individual plates. Finely shred remaining lettuce; mound atop leaves. Divide soy sauce among 6 tiny dipping bowls; add 1/2 teaspoon of the horseradish to each, then place bowls on plates. Place a few lemon wedges on each plate.

4 Cut chicken crosswise into 1/2-inch-wide strips. Spoon rice and chicken over lettuce; sprinkle with onions. To eat, squeeze lemon into soy mixture. Dip chicken into sauce. Or tear lettuce leaves into pieces and fill with chicken, rice, and shredded lettuce; season with sauce and eat out of hand.

makes 6 servings

per serving: 360 calories, 44 g protein, 35 g carbohydrates, 3 g total fat, 99 mg cholesterol, 742 mg sodium

apple turkey loaf

preparation time: about 25 minutes
baking time: about 1 hour

1 **tablespoon butter or margarine**

2 **medium-size tart green-skinned apples, cored and chopped**

1 **medium-size onion, chopped**

1 1/2 **pounds ground skinless turkey breast**

1 1/2 **teaspoons dry marjoram**

1 **teaspoon** *each* **dry thyme, dry sage, and pepper**

1/2 **cup chopped parsley**

2 **large egg whites (about** 1/4 **cup)**

1/2 **cup** *each* **fine dry bread crumbs and nonfat milk**

1 Melt butter in a wide frying pan over medium heat. Add apples and onion. Cook, stirring occasionally, until onion is soft (about 7 minutes). Remove from heat and let cool; then spoon into a large bowl. Add turkey, marjoram, thyme, sage, pepper, parsley, egg whites, bread crumbs, and milk; mix lightly.

2 Pat turkey mixture into a 5- by 9-inch loaf pan. Bake in a 350° oven until browned on top and no longer pink in center; cut to test (about 1 hour). Drain and discard fat from pan, then invert pan and turn loaf out onto a platter. Serve loaf hot; or let cool, then cover and refrigerate for up to 1 day.

makes 6 servings

per serving: 237 calories, 32 g protein, 19 g carbohydrates, 3 g total fat, 76 mg cholesterol, 185 mg sodium

grilled game hens with jalapeño jelly glaze

preparation time: 40 to 50 minutes

3 Rock Cornish game hens (1½ lbs. *each*), thawed if frozen

1 tablespoon butter or margarine

¼ cup jalapeño jelly

2 teaspoons lime juice

1 Using poultry scissors, cut each game hen in half through backbone and breastbone. Remove giblets and reserve for other uses. Rinse hens and pat dry.

2 In a small pan, combine butter and jelly; stir over medium-high heat until melted. Remove from heat and stir in lime juice.

3 Place hen halves, skin side up, on a barbecue grill 4 to 6 inches above a solid bed of medium-hot coals. Grill, turning several times and basting with jelly mixture during last 15 minutes, until hens are browned and breast meat in thickest portion is no longer pink when slashed (30 to 40 minutes).

makes 6 servings

per serving: 338 calories, 43 g protein, 9 g carbohydrates, 13 g total fat, 202 mg cholesterol, 26 mg sodium

chicken with black bean sauce

preparation time: about 40 minutes

1 teaspoon *each* cornstarch and soy sauce

4 teaspoons water

2 teaspoons dry sherry

1 whole chicken breast (about 1 lb.), skinned, boned, and cut into bite-size pieces

3½ tablespoons salad oil

Cooking Sauce (recipe follows)

1 pound red or green bell peppers or 1 pound asparagus

2 teaspoons fermented salted black beans, rinsed, drained, and finely chopped

1 large clove garlic, minced

1 medium-size onion, cut into wedges, layers separated

1 In a bowl, stir together cornstarch, soy, 1 teaspoon of the water, and sherry. Add chicken and stir to coat; then stir in 1½ teaspoons of the oil and let marinate for 15 minutes.

2 Meanwhile, prepare Cooking Sauce; set aside. Seed bell peppers and cut into 1-inch squares. (Or snap off and discard tough ends of asparagus; cut spears into ½-inch slanting slices.)

3 Place a wok over high heat; when wok is hot, add 2 tablespoons of the oil. When oil begins to heat, add black beans and garlic; stir once. Add chicken mixture and stir-fry until meat is no longer pink in center; cut to test (about 3 minutes). Remove from wok and set aside.

4 Pour remaining 1 tablespoon oil into wok; when oil is hot, add bell peppers and onion and stir-fry for 1 minute. Add remaining 1 table-spoon water and cook, uncovered, until vegetables are tender-crisp to bite—2 to 4 more minutes. (If using asparagus, add 2 tablespoons water; cook, covered, for 3 to 4 minutes.) Return chicken to wok. Stir Cooking Sauce, pour into wok, and stir until sauce boils and thickens.

COOKING SAUCE

Stir together 1 tablespoon *each* soy sauce and cornstarch, ¼ teaspoon sugar, and ½ cup regular-strength chicken broth or water.

makes 2 or 3 servings

per serving: 320 calories, 25 g protein, 14 g carbohydrates, 18 g total fat, 57 mg cholesterol, 791 mg sodium

turkey chili

preparation time: about 55 minutes

1 tablespoon salad oil

1 pound skinned and boned turkey breast, cut into 1 1/2-inch chunks

1 medium-size onion, chopped

1 small green bell pepper, seeded and chopped

1 clove garlic, minced or pressed

1 small can (about 8 oz.) tomatoes, drained and chopped

2 cans (about 15 oz. *each*) kidney beans, drained

1 large can (15 oz.) no-salt-added tomato sauce

2 tablespoons reduced-sodium soy sauce

1 1/2 tablespoons chili powder

1/2 teaspoon *each* ground cumin, dry sage leaves, and dry thyme leaves

Garnishes (optional; suggestions follow)

1 Heat oil in a 12- to 14-inch frying pan over medium heat. Add turkey and cook, stirring often, until browned on all sides (about 6 minutes).

2 Remove turkey from pan. Add onion, bell pepper, and garlic; cook, stirring occasionally, until onion is soft (about 10 minutes). Add tomatoes, beans, tomato sauce, soy, chili powder, cumin, sage, and thyme. Bring to a boil. Then reduce heat, cover, and simmer until chili is thick and meat is no longer pink in center; cut to test (about 20 minutes; uncover for last 5 minutes).

3 Serve in bowls and accompany with garnishes.

makes 4 servings

GARNISHES

In separate bowls, offer 8 green onions (including tops), sliced; 1 cup chopped tomatoes; and 1/2 cup shredded jack cheese, if desired.

per serving: 407 calories, 40g protein, 47g carbohydrates, 7g total fat, 70 mg cholesterol, 1259 mg sodium

chicken kebabs shanghai

preparation time: about 40 minutes
marinating time: at least 30 minutes

3/4 teaspoon grated orange peel

1/3 cup orange juice

3 tablespoons firmly packed brown sugar

2 tablespoons reduced-sodium soy sauce

4 teaspoons *each* minced fresh ginger and red wine vinegar

1 tablespoon Asian sesame oil or salad oil

1/2 teaspoon ground coriander

1 1/2 pounds skinned, boned chicken breasts, cut into 1 1/2-inch chunks

1 medium-size pineapple, peeled, cored, and cut into 1-inch chunks

1 In a medium-size bowl, mix orange peel, orange juice, sugar, soy sauce, ginger, vinegar, oil, and coriander. Stir in chicken. Cover and refrigerate for at least 30 minutes or up to 2 hours.

2 Lift chicken from marinade and drain briefly; reserve marinade. Thread chicken and pineapple chunks on thin metal skewers, alternating 2 chicken chunks and one pineapple chunk. Brush reserved marinade over pineapple. Place skewers on a rack in a 12- by 15-inch broiler pan. Broil about 4 inches below heat, turning once, until chicken is no longer pink in center; cut to test (about 12 minutes).

makes 4 to 6 servings

per serving: 299 calories, 33 g protein, 319 carbohydrates, 5 g total fat, 79 mg cholesterol, 333 mg sodium

picadillo stew

preparation time: about 40 minutes

2 tablespoons slivered almonds

1/4 cup dry red wine

2 tablespoons reduced sodium soy sauce

1 tablespoon lemon juice

2 teaspoons sugar

1 teaspoon *each* ground cumin, ground coriander, and chili powder

1/8 teaspoon ground cinnamon

4 teaspoons cornstarch

1 teaspoon salad oil

1 pound boneless turkey breast, cut into 1-inch chunks

1 large onion, chopped

2 cloves garlic, minced or pressed

1 can (about 14 1/2 oz.) tomatoes

2/3 cup raisins

Pepper

1 Toast almonds in a small flying pan over medium heat until golden (5 to 7 minutes), stirring often. Transfer almonds to a bowl and set aside.

2 In a small bowl, mix wine, soy sauce, lemon juice, sugar, cumin, coriander, chili powder, cinnamon, and cornstarch until smooth. Set aside.

3 Heat oil in a wide nonstick frying pan or 5-quart pan over high heat. Add turkey, onion, and garlic. Cook, stirring, until meat is no longer pink in thickest part; cut to test (10 to 15 minutes). Add water, 1 tablespoon at a time, if pan appears dry. Add tomatoes and their liquid (break tomatoes up with a spoon), wine mixture, and raisins to pan. Bring to a boil; boil, stirring, just until thickened.

4 To serve, ladle stew into bowls and sprinkle with almonds. Season to taste with pepper.

makes 4 servings

per serving: 317 calories, 32 g protein, 36 g carbohydrates, 5 g total fat, 70 mg cholesterol, 538 mg sodium

strawberry chicken

preparation time: about 10 minutes
baking time: about 45 minutes

1 can (about 8 oz.) tomato sauce

1 cup strawberry jam

2 tablespoons red wine vinegar

1 tablespoon chili powder

1/2 teaspoon *each* dry thyme and ground ginger

12 skinless chicken thighs (2 to 2 1/4 lbs. *total*) trimmed of fat

Salt

3 cups hot cooked a short-grain rice

1/2 cup thinly sliced green onions

1 In a shallow 3-quart casserole, mix tomato sauce, jam, vinegar, chili powder, thyme, and ginger.

2 Rinse chicken and pat dry; then add to sauce and turn to coat. Bake in a 400° oven, basting occasionally, until meat near bone is no longer pink; cut to test (about 45 minutes). Season to taste with salt.

3 Spoon rice onto a platter. Top with chicken, sauce, and onions.

makes 4 to 6 servings

per serving: 505 calories, 33 g protein, 81 g carbohydrates, 6 g total fat, 118 mg cholesterol, 441 mg sodium

chicken in a squash shell

preparation time: about 1 hour

Nonstick cooking spray

2 small acorn squash

Soy-Ginger Sauce (recipe follows)

1 tablespoon salad oil

1 pound boneless and skinless chicken breasts, cut into $1/2$-inch cubes

$1/2$ cup *each* finely diced red bell pepper and jicama

1 small onion, finely chopped

2 small firm-ripe tomatoes, peeled and finely diced

1 teaspoon Szechuan peppercorns, coarsely ground, or $1/2$ teaspoon pepper

$1/4$ cup chopped green onions (including tops)

Plain lowfat yogurt (optional)

1 Lightly coat a 9- by 13-inch baking pan with cooking spray. With a sharp, heavy knife, cut squash in half lengthwise and scoop out seeds. Arrange squash, cut sides down, in pan. Bake in a 400° oven until tender when pierced (about 40 minutes).

2 Meanwhile, prepare Soy-Ginger Sauce and set aside.

3 About 15 minutes before squash is done, heat oil in a wide frying pan or wok over medium-high heat. Add chicken and cook, stirring, until meat in center is no longer pink; cut to test (2 to 3 minutes). Lift out with a slotted spoon and set aside. Add bell pepper, jicama, onion, tomatoes, and peppercorns to pan; cook, stirring, for 5 minutes. Add sauce; boil until thickened. Return chicken and any juices to pan, remove from heat, and keep warm.

4 Place squash in individual bowls and fill with chicken mixture. Sprinkle with green onions. Offer with yogurt, if desired.

makes 4 servings

SOY-GINGER SAUCE

Stir together 2 tablespoons each reduced-sodium soy sauce and dry sherry, $3/4$ cup low-sodium chicken broth, 1 tablespoon each cornstarch and firmly packed brown sugar, and 1 teaspoon finely minced fresh ginger.

per serving: 282 calories, 29 g protein, 30 g carbohydrates, 6 g total fat, 66 mg cholesterol, 396 mg sodium

chicken enchilada bake

preparation time: about 50 minutes

12 corn tortillas (7-inch diameter)

5 medium-size tomatoes, peeled and thinly sliced

2 cups skinless and boneless shredded cooked chicken breast

1 cup thinly sliced green onions (including tops)

1 tablespoon margarine

2 tablespoons all-purpose flour

2 cups low-sodium chicken broth

1 cup plain lowfat yogurt

1 can (4 oz.) diced green chiles

2 ounces (about $1/2$ cup) grated Cheddar cheese

1 Dip tortillas, one at a time, in water; let drain briefly. Stack and cut into 8 wedges. Spread a third of the tortillas in a 9- by 13-inch baking pan. Top with half the tomatoes; cover with half the chicken and onions. Repeat layers, ending with tortillas. Set aside.

2 In a 2- to 3-quart pan, melt margarine over medium heat. Add flour and cook, stirring, for 20 seconds. Whisk in chicken broth and bring to a boil. Remove from heat and add yogurt and chiles, whisking until smooth. Pour over tortilla mixture.

3 Cover and bake in a 375° oven for 20 minutes. Remove cover, sprinkle with Cheddar, and continue baking, uncovered, until cheese is melted (about 10 more minutes).

makes 8 servings

per serving: 254 calories, 19 g protein, 28 g carbohydrates, 8 g total fat, 39 mg cholesterol, 293 mg sodium

turkey curry with soba

preparation time: about 50 minutes

1 tablespoon salad oil

1 pound boneless, skinless turkey breast, cut into 1¹/₂-inch chunks

1 large onion, thinly sliced

1 clove garlic, minced or pressed

1 tablespoon grated fresh ginger

1 teaspoon *each* crushed red pepper flakes, ground coriander, ground cumin, and ground turmeric

¹/₂ teaspoon fennel seeds

1 cup low-sodium chicken broth

1 package (about 7 oz.) dry soba noodles

1 cup plain nonfat yogurt

¹/₄ cup unsalted dry-roasted cashews

1 Heat oil in a wide frying pan over medium heat. Add turkey and cook, stirring often, until browned on all sides (about 6 minutes). Using a slotted spoon, remove turkey from pan.

2 Add onion and garlic to pan; cook, stirring occasionally, until onion is soft (about 10 minutes). Add ginger, red pepper flakes, coriander, cumin, turmeric, and fennel seeds; cook, stirring, for 1 minute.

3 Return turkey to pan. Add broth and bring to a boil. Then reduce heat, cover, and simmer until meat is no longer pink in center; cut to test (about 20 minutes). Remove from heat.

4 While turkey is simmering, cook noodles in boiling water according to package directions until just tender to bite; drain well and pour into a large, shallow serving bowl.

5 Stir yogurt into turkey mixture, then pour mixture over noodles. Sprinkle with cashews.

makes 6 servings

per serving: 294 calories, 6 g total fat, 34 g carbohydrates, 27 g protein, 48 mg cholesterol, 340 mg sodium

turkey & lima bean stew

preparation time: about 20 minutes
cooking time: about 1 hour

1 large onion, chopped

2 cups sliced mushrooms

1 cup thinly sliced carrots

1 teaspoon dry thyme

3 cups low-sodium chicken broth

2 tablespoons lemon juice

2 pounds boneless, skinless turkey or chicken thighs, trimmed of fat and cut into 1-inch chunks

1 tablespoon cornstarch

1 package (about 10 oz.) frozen baby lima beans, thawed

1 In a 5- to 6-quart pan, combine onion, mushrooms, carrots, thyme, and 1 cup of the broth. Bring to a boil over high heat; then boil, stirring occasionally, until liquid evaporates and vegetables begin to brown (about 10 minutes). To deglaze, add ¹/₄ cup more broth and stir to scrape browned bits free. Then continue to cook, stirring occasionally, until vegetables begin to brown again. Repeat deglazing and browning steps, using ¹/₄ cup more broth each time, until vegetable mixture is richly browned. Then deglaze one last time with lemon juice.

2 Stir turkey and ¹/₂ cup more broth into vegetable mixture. Bring to a boil over high heat. Then reduce heat to low, cover, and simmer until turkey chunks are no longer pink in center; cut to test (about 40 minutes; about 25 minutes for chicken). Skim and discard fat from sauce.

3 Smoothly blend cornstarch with ³/₄ cup of the broth. Add cornstarch mixture and beans to pan; bring to a boil over medium-high heat, stirring. Continue to boil, stirring, until beans are tender to bite.

makes 6 servings

per serving: 299 calories, 36 g protein, 20 g carbohydrates, 7 g total fat, 114 mg cholesterol, 182 mg sodium

kung pao chicken

preparation time: about 50 minutes

1 cup long-grain white rice

Cooking Sauce (recipe follows)

1 1/2 cups Chinese pea pods (also called snow or sugar peas) or sugar snap peas, ends and strings removed

1 tablespoon cornstarch

1 tablespoon dry white wine

1/2 teaspoon sugar

1 pound boneless, skinless chicken breast, cut into 3/4-inch chunks

2 cloves garlic, minced or pressed

1 cup peeled, shredded jicama

2 tablespoons salted roasted peanuts, chopped

1 In a 3- to 4-quart pan, bring 2 cups water to a boil over high heat; stir in rice. Reduce heat, cover, and simmer until liquid has been absorbed and rice is tender to bite (about 20 minutes). Meanwhile, prepare Cooking Sauce; set aside. Cut pea pods diagonally into 3/4-inch pieces; set aside.

2 In a large bowl, dissolve cornstarch in wine; stir in sugar. Add chicken and stir to coat. Then turn chicken mixture into a wide nonstick frying pan or wok; add garlic and 1 tablespoon water. Stir-fry over medium-high heat until meat is no longer pink in center; cut to test (4 to 6 minutes). Remove from pan with a slotted spoon and keep warm.

3 Add pea pods, jicama, and 1 tablespoon water to pan; stir-fry until pea pods are tender-crisp to bite (about 1 minute). Stir Cooking Sauce well; pour into pan and bring to a boil. Remove from heat and stir in chicken.

4 Spoon rice onto a rimmed platter; top with chicken mixture and sprinkle with peanuts.

makes 4 servings

COOKING SAUCE

Mix 1 tablespoon each sugar and chili paste with garlic; 1 tablespoon unseasoned rice vinegar or distilled white vinegar; and 1 tablespoon *each* hoisin sauce and Asian sesame oil.

per serving: 425 calories, 33 g protein, 51 g carbohydrates, 9 g total fat, 66 mg cholesterol, 122 mg sodium

lemon turkey scaloppine

preparation time: about 25 minutes

1 pound skinned and boned turkey breast, sliced 1/2 inch thick

2 tablespoons all-purpose flour

1 tablespoon salad oil

1/2 cup lemon juice

2 tablespoons drained capers

1 lemon, thinly sliced

1 Rinse turkey, pat dry, and cut into serving-size pieces. Place between sheets of plastic wrap. With a flat-surfaced mallet, pound turkey to a thickness of about 1/4 inch. Dust with flour.

2 Heat oil in a 12- to 14-inch frying pan over medium-high heat. Add turkey and cook, turning once, until golden brown on both sides (about 4 minutes). With a slotted spoon, transfer turkey to a platter; keep warm.

3 Add lemon juice and capers to pan. Bring to a boil and cook, stirring, until thickened (about 2 minutes). Pour sauce over turkey; garnish with lemon slices.

makes 4 servings

per serving: 186 calories, 27 g protein, 8 g carbohydrates, 5 g total fat, 70 mg cholesterol, 193 mg sodium

chicken yakitori

preparation time: about 1 hour
marinating time: 1 to 8 hours

2 tablespoons sesame seeds

**3 whole chicken breasts (about 1 lb. *each*),
skinned, boned, and split**

Sherry-Soy Marinade (recipe follows)

6 medium-size Asian eggplants

**18 large fresh shiitake mushrooms or regular
button mushrooms**

1 In a small frying pan, toast sesame seeds over medium heat, shaking pan often, until golden (about 3 minutes). Set aside.

2 Cut each breast half into 6 equal-size chunks; place in a medium-size bowl, Prepare Sherry-Soy Marinade. Pour ¼ cup of the marinade over chicken, turning gently to coat; reserve remaining marinade. Cover and refrigerate chicken and reserved marinade separately for at least 1 hour or up to 8 hours.

3 Lift chicken from marinade and let drain briefly, discarding marinade in bowl. Thread chicken on skewers. Set aside.

4 Evenly slash each eggplant lengthwise in 4 or 5 places, making cuts about ⅓ inch deep. Cut mush room stems flush with caps. Place eggplants on a lightly greased grill 4 to 6 inches above a solid bed of hot coals. Cook, turning often, until very soft when pressed (about 35 minutes).

5 About 20 minutes before eggplants are done, dip mushrooms in reserved marinade, drain briefly, and place on grill. Cook, turning once, until lightly browned (about 10 minutes total). Meanwhile, place chicken on grill and cook, turning occasionally, until meat in center is no longer pink; cut to test (10 to 12 minutes).

6 Arrange chicken and vegetables on separate platters. Moisten with some of the remaining marinade and sprinkle with sesame seeds. Offer with remaining marinade.

makes 6 servings

SHERRY-SOY MARINADE

Stir together ⅓ cup dry sherry, 3 tablespoons *each* sesame oil and reduced sodium soy sauce, and 1 ½ teaspoons finely minced fresh ginger.

per serving: 295 calories, 39 g protein, 16 g carbohydrates, 9 g total fat, 86 mg cholesterol, 332 mg sodium

chicken chutney burgers

preparation time: about 15 minutes

²/₃ cup Major Grey chutney, large pieces chopped

1 ¹/₂ tablespoons lemon juice

1 tablespoon Dijon mustard

³/₄ pound ground chicken

¹/₄ cup sliced green onion

¹/₂ teaspoon ground cumin

8 slices (*each* ¹/₂ in. thick) sourdough French bread

4 thin slices red onion

20 pre-washed spinach leaves

1 Combine chutney, lemon juice, and mustard; set two-thirds of mixture aside. Combine remaining chutney mixture with chicken, green onion, and cumin. Shape into 4 patties, each about 4 inches wide, and place on a rack in a broiler pan. Broil 3 inches below heat until well browned on both sides, turning as needed (6 to 7 minutes).

2 Meanwhile, brown bread in a toaster, then spread one side of each slice with reserved chutney mixture.

3 Separate red onion into rings and place between bread with burgers and spinach.

makes 4 servings

per serving: 387 calories, 23 g protein, 61 g carbohydrates, 4 g total fat, 60 mg cholesterol, 948 mg sodium

ground turkey chili mole

preparation time: about 1 hour

1 medium-size onion, chopped

1 pound ground skinless turkey

2 cloves garlic, minced or pressed

1 can (about 8 oz.) tomato sauce

1 can (about 14 ¹/₂ oz.) stewed tomatoes

1 can (about 15 oz.) red kidney beans, drained and rinsed; or 2 cups cooked red kidney beans, drained and rinsed

1 tablespoon molasses

¹/₄ teaspoon liquid hot pepper seasoning

1 tablespoon unsweetened cocoa

1 teaspoon *each* paprika and ground cumin

¹/₂ teaspoon *each* dry oregano and dry basil

1 In a 4- to 5-quart pan, combine onion and ¹/₄ cup water. Bring to a boil over medium-high heat; then boil, stirring occasionally, until liquid evaporates and onion begins to brown (about 5 minutes). To deglaze, add ¹/₄ cup more water and stir to scrape browned bits free. Then continue to cook, stirring occasionally, until onion begins to brown again. Repeat deglazing and browning steps, using ¹/₄ cup more water.

2 Crumble turkey into pan; add garlic. Cook, stirring, until meat is no longer pink and liquid has evaporated. Stir in tomato sauce, tomatoes, beans, molasses, hot pepper seasoning, cocoa, paprika, cumin, oregano, and basil. Bring to a boil; reduce heat, cover, and simmer until flavors are well blended (about 30 minutes).

makes 4 to 6 servings

per serving: 256 calories, 22 g protein, 25 g carbohydrates, 8 g total fat, 66 mg cholesterol, 685 mg sodium

chicken and apple stir-fry

preparation time: about 35 minutes

4 teaspoons butter or margarine

2 large tart apples, peeled, cored, and cut into
¼-inch-thick slices

1 pound skinless, boneless chicken breast, cut into
½- by 2-inch strips

1 large onion, finely chopped

⅔ cup dry sherry or apple juice

½ cup half-and-half

1 Melt 1 tablespoon of the butter in a wide nonstick frying pan or wok over medium heat. Add apples and stir-fry just until tender to bite (about 2 minutes). Remove apples from pan with a slotted spoon and keep warm.

2 Increase heat to medium-high and melt remaining 1 teaspoon butter in pan. Add chicken and stir-fry until no longer pink in center; cut to test (3 to 4 minutes). Remove chicken from pan with a slotted spoon and keep warm.

3 Add onion and 2 tablespoons of the sherry to pan; stir-fry until onion is soft (about 3 minutes). Add remaining sherry and bring to a boil; boil, stirring, for 1 minute. Add half-and-half and boil, stirring, until sauce is slightly thickened (about 2 minutes). Return apples and chicken to pan and mix gently but thoroughly.

makes 4 servings

per serving: 309 calories, 28 g protein, 21 g carbohydrates, 8 g total fat, 84 mg cholesterol, 126 mg sodium

braised chicken with green chile sauce

preparation time: about 55 minutes

1 large onion, chopped

2 cloves garlic, minced or pressed

1 cup low-sodium chicken broth

1 teaspoon dry oregano

½ teaspoon ground cumin

1 tablespoon red wine vinegar

3 pounds boneless, skinless chicken or turkey
thighs, trimmed of fat and cut into 1-inch chunks

2 large green bell peppers, seeded and chopped

½ cup chopped cilantro

1 large can (about 7 oz.) diced green chiles

Salt and pepper

Hot cooked rice or warm flour tortillas

Tomato wedges, plain nonfat yogurt or reduced-
fat sour cream, and lime wedges

1 In a 5- to 6-quart pan, combine onion, garlic, broth, oregano, and cumin. Bring to a boil over high heat; boil, stirring occasionally, until liquid evaporates and onion begins to brown (about 10 minutes). To deglaze, add 2 tablespoons water and stir to scrape browned bits free. Then continue to cook, stirring occasionally, until onion begins to brown again. Repeat deglazing and browning steps, using 2 tablespoons water each time, until onion is richly browned. Then deglaze one last time with vinegar and 1 tablespoon water.

2 Stir in chicken, bell peppers, cilantro, chiles, and 1 tablespoon water. Cover and cook over low heat, stirring often, until chicken chunks are no longer pink in center; cut to test (about 15 minutes). Skim and discard fat from sauce; season to taste with salt and pepper.

3 Spoon chicken mixture into a bowl. Serve over rice; offer tomato wedges, yogurt, and lime wedges to season each serving.

makes 6 to 8 servings

per serving: 273 calories, 40 g protein, 9 g carbohydrates, 8 g total fat, 161 mg cholesterol, 351 mg sodium

lemon chicken

preparation time: about 30 minutes

5 or 6 large lemons

³/₄ cup plus 1 tablespoon cornstarch

¹/₃ cup fat-free reduced-sodium chicken broth

¹/₄ cup sugar

2 tablespoons light corn syrup

2 tablespoons distilled white vinegar

1 tablespoon plus 1 teaspoon vegetable oil

¹/₂ teaspoon salt (optional)

2 cloves garlic, minced or pressed

2 large egg whites

¹/₄ cup all-purpose flour

1 teaspoon baking powder

1 teaspoon finely minced fresh ginger

¹/₈ teaspoon ground white pepper

1 pound skinless, boneless chicken breast, cut
   into ¹/₂- by 3-inch strips

Finely shredded lemon peel

Cilantro sprigs

1 To prepare sauce, finely shred enough peel (colored part only) from 1 or 2 of the lemons to make ¹/₂ teaspoon; set aside. Squeeze enough juice to measure 3 tablespoons. In a small bowl, stir together lemon juice and 1 tablespoon of the cornstarch until blended. Stir in lemon peel, broth, sugar, corn syrup, vinegar, 1 tablespoon water, 1 teaspoon of the oil, ¹/₄ teaspoon of the salt (if using), and garlic. Set sauce aside.

2 Thinly slice the remaining lemons and place slices on a rimmed platter, overlapping them, if necessary; cover and set aside.

3 In a large bowl, beat egg whites and ¹/₂ cup water to blend. Add remaining ³/₄ cup cornstarch, flour, baking powder, ginger, remaining ¹/₄ teaspoon salt (if using), and white pepper; stir until smoothly blended.

4 Heat remaining 1 tablespoon oil in a wide nonstick frying pan or wok over medium-high heat. Meanwhile, dip chicken pieces in egg-white batter. Lift out and drain briefly to let excess batter drip off; discard remaining batter.

5 When oil is hot, add chicken and stir-fry gently, separating pieces, until meat is lightly browned on outside and no longer pink in center; cut to test (5 to 7 minutes; if any pieces brown too much, remove them from pan and keep warm). Arrange chicken over lemon slices on platter; keep warm.

6 Wipe pan clean (be careful; pan is hot). Stir reserved lemon sauce well; pour into pan. Stir over medium-high heat until sauce boils and thickens slightly (1 to 2 minutes). Pour sauce over chicken and sprinkle with additional shredded lemon peel. Garnish with cilantro sprigs.

makes 4 servings

per serving: 368 calories, 30 g protein, 56 g carbohydrates, 6 g total fat, 66 mg cholesterol, 245 mg sodium

THAWING CHICKEN IN THE MICROWAVE: Unwrap a frozen 3- to 3 ¹/₂- pound cut-up chicken, then place on a microwave-safe plate; cover loosely with heavy-duty plastic wrap. Microwave on MEDIUM (50%) for 10 minutes, turning chicken over and giving plate a quarter turn after 5 minutes. Let stand for 10 minutes. Repeat, microwaving and standing; as soon as possible, separate pieces and arrange in a single layer, with meatiest portions toward edge of plate. Wings should be thawed after second 10-minute period. Microwave remaining pieces on MEDIUM (50%) for 5 more minutes; let stand for 5 minutes. If needed, microwave on MEDIUM (50%) for 2 more minutes. Thawed chicken should be flexible, but still very cold.

seafood

sautéed hoisin shrimp

preparation time: about 25 minutes

3 tablespoons hoisin sauce

2 tablespoons *each* unseasoned rice vinegar
   and water

2 teaspoons sugar

½ teaspoon *each* ground ginger and cornstarch

⅛ teaspoon crushed red pepper flakes

2 tablespoons salad oil

1 pound medium-size raw shrimp
   (30 to 32 per lb.), shelled and deveined

1 clove garlic, minced or pressed

6 green onions (including tops),
   cut diagonally into 1-inch lengths

BUYING FRESH FISH Always buy the freshest fish you can find. The flesh of whole fish should spring back when gently pressed, and the eyes should be clear and full, not sunken. Fillets and steaks should look cleanly cut and feel firm and moist. Avoid any fish with a strong, unpleasant odor; truly fresh seafood has a mild and delicate aroma. Uncooked fish doesn't keep well. To avoid waste, buy only as much as you need, and cook it as soon as possible after purchase—preferably on the same day, within 2 days at the most. To store fish, discard the market wrapping; rinse the fish under cook running water, place it in a container, and cover with wet paper towels. Store in the coldest part of your refrigerator.

1 In a bowl, mix hoisin sauce, vinegar, water, sugar, ginger, cornstarch, and red pepper flakes; set aside.

2 Heat oil in a wide frying pan or wok over medium-high heat. Add shrimp and garlic and cook, stirring occasionally, for about 2 minutes. Add onions and hoisin mixture and continue to cook, stirring, until sauce is thickened and shrimp are just opaque in center; cut to test (about 3 more minutes).

makes 4 servings

per serving: 192 calories, 20 g protein, 9 g carbohydrates, 9 g total fat, 140 mg cholesterol, 520 mg sodium

broiled prawns wrapped in bacon

preparation time: about 40 minutes

8 slices bacon

16 jumbo raw shrimp (16 to 20 per lb.)

1 Soak eight 10-inch-long bamboo skewers in hot water to cover for about 30 minutes.

2 Meanwhile, in a wide frying pan, cook bacon over medium heat until some of the fat has cooked out and bacon begins to brown (3 to 4 minutes); bacon should not be crisp. Drain, then cut each slice in half lengthwise.

3 Shell shrimp (leave tails on) and devein. Wrap a bacon half-slice around each shrimp. Thread shrimp on pairs of skewers. Then place on rack of a broiler pan and broil about 4 inches below heat, turning once, until bacon is golden brown and shrimp are just opaque in center; cut to test (6 to 10 minutes).

makes 4 servings

per serving: 170 calories, 23 g protein, 0.9 g carbohydrates, 8 g total fat, 151 mg cholesterol, 338 mg sodium

grilled lobster with potato salad

preparation time: about 45 minutes

1½ pounds Yukon Gold potatoes, peeled

⅓ cup thawed frozen orange juice concentrate

¼ cup lemon juice

4 teaspoons Dijon mustard

⅔ cup finely chopped green onions, including tops

Salt

4 spiny or rock lobster tails (½ lb. *each*), thawed if frozen

¼ cup fresh salmon caviar (ikura optional)

1 In a 5- to 6-quart pan over high heat, bring potatoes and 3 quarts water to a boil. Cover and simmer until potatoes are tender when pierced, 30 to 35 minutes. Drain. When potatoes are cool enough to touch, cut into ¼-inch chunks.

2 Meanwhile, in a large bowl, stir together orange juice concentrate, lemon juice, Dijon mustard, and green onions. Add potato chunks and mix gently. Add salt to taste.

3 With scissors, cut lengthwise down the center of the top of each lobster shell. Set each tail, underside down, on a cutting board. Force a heavy knife through the cut in each shell to slice each lobster tail in half. Rinse lobster in shell.

4 Have barbecue ready with direct heat at hot. Lightly oil grill and lay lobster on it. Turn once and cook evenly until lobster is opaque and moist-looking in center of thickest (cut to test), about 7 minutes.

5 Mound potato salad equally on plates; top with caviar. Place 2 lobster halves around each salad portion.

makes 4 servings

per serving: 297 calories, 29 g protein, 40 g carbohydrate, 1.1 g total fat, 90 mg cholesterol, 613 mg sodium

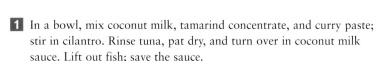

tuna with coconut-curry sauce

preparation time: about 25 minutes

1 cup canned coconut milk

4 teaspoons tamarind concentrate or lime juice

**1½ teaspoons Thai red curry paste
or curry powder**

2 tablespoons minced fresh cilantro

1½ pounds boned tuna (ahi, 1¼ to 1½ in. thick)

½ cup chopped salted roasted cashews

4 cups hot cooked rice

¼ cup slivered fresh basil leaves

Salt

1 In a bowl, mix coconut milk, tamarind concentrate, and curry paste; stir in cilantro. Rinse tuna, pat dry, and turn over in coconut milk sauce. Lift out fish; save the sauce.

2 Pour sauce into a 1- to 1 ½-quart pan; bring to a boil over high heat, stirring. Or bring to a boil in a microwave-safe container in a microwave oven at full power (100%). Keep warm.

3 Have barbecue ready with direct heat at very hot. Lightly oil grill and set fish on it. Cook tuna until bottom is pale color about ¼ inch into fish (cut to test; center is red), about 2 minutes. Turn tuna with a wide spatula and cook until side on grill is the same color as it is on the top, and center is still pink to red, about 1 minute longer.

4 Stir cashews into rice, spoon onto plates, and top with equal portions tuna. Sprinkle with basil. Serve with warm coconut-curry sauce and add salt to taste.

makes 4 servings

per serving: 610 calories, 48 g protein, 52 g carbohydrates, 23 g total fat, 77 mg cholesterol, 251 mg sodium

shrimp sauté

preparation time: about 40 minutes

2 teaspoons butter or margarine

½ cup finely chopped celery

⅓ cup finely chopped shallots

2 cloves garlic, minced or pressed

**1 medium-size red bell pepper,
seeded and finely chopped**

1¼ cups fat-free reduced-sodium chicken broth

**1 pound large raw shrimp (31 to 35 per lb.),
shelled and deveined**

**⅔ cup fruity white wine,
such as Johannisberg Riesling**

1 Melt butter in a wide nonstick frying pan or wok over medium-high heat. Add celery, shallots, garlic, bell pepper, and broth. Cook, stirring often, until liquid evaporates (about 10 minutes).

2 Add shrimp to pan and stir-fry until just opaque in center; cut to test (3 to 4 minutes). Remove shrimp from pan with tongs or a slotted spoon; place in a serving bowl and keep warm. Add wine to pan and bring to a boil; then boil, stirring often, until liquid is reduced by about two-thirds (about 7 minutes). Spoon sauce over shrimp.

makes 4 servings

per serving: 140 calories, 20 g protein, 6 g carbohydrates, 4 g total fat, 145 mg cholesterol, 374 mg sodium

swordfish steaks with salsa

preparation time: about 25 minutes

4 swordfish steaks (*each* about 1 inch thick)

2 tablespoons salad oil

2 cloves garlic, minced or pressed

1 fresh jalapeño or other small hot chile, stemmed, seeded, and minced

5 firm-ripe pear-shaped tomatoes, seeded and diced

1/2 cup packed fresh cilantro leaves, chopped

1 Rinse fish and pat dry. Heat oil in a wide frying pan over medium-high heat.

2 Add fish and cook, turning once, until well browned on outside and just opaque but still moist in thickest part; cut to test (8 to 10 minutes). Transfer to a warm platter; keep warm.

3 Add garlic and chile to pan and cook, stirring, until fragrant (about 30 seconds). Add tomatoes and cilantro and cook, stirring, until hot (about 2 minutes). Spoon over fish.

makes 4 servings

per serving: 349 calories, 46 g protein, 3 g carbohydrates, 16 g total fat, 89 mg cholesterol, 209 mg sodium

grilled fish steaks

preparation time: about 15 minutes

Dill Butter (recipe follows)

4 salmon, tuna, swordfish, halibut, or sturgeon steaks (*each* about 1 inch thick)

Olive oil or salad oil

Salt and pepper

1 Prepare Dill Butter. Set aside.

2 Rinse fish, pat dry, and rub with oil. Place on a lightly greased grill 4 to 6 inches above a solid bed of hot coals. Cook, turning once or twice, until fish is just opaque (or tuna is slightly pink) but still moist in thickest part; cut to test (8 to 10 minutes).

3 Season fish to taste with salt and pepper; offer Dill Butter to spoon over individual portions.

DILL BUTTER

In a small bowl, mix 1/4 cup butter or margarine (at room temperature) and 1/4 cup chopped fresh dill (or 2 tablespoons dry dill weed) until well blended. Makes about 1/4 cup.

makes 4 servings

per serving of fish: 272 calories, 34 g protein, 0 g carbohydrates, 14 g total fat, 94 mg cholesterol, 75 mg sodium

per tablespoon of Dill Butter: 106 calories, 0.4 g protein, 0.9 g carbohydrates, 12 g total fat, 31 mg cholesterol, 120 mg sodium

baby salmon with sautéed leeks

preparation time: about 40 minutes

About 1½ pounds leeks, roots and most of dark green tops trimmed

¼ cup butter or margarine

½ teaspoon dry thyme

2 tablespoons lemon juice

Salt and ground white pepper

6 boned baby salmon or trout (about ½ lb. *each***), heads removed**

1 Split leeks lengthwise and rinse well; then thinly slice crosswise (you should have about 3 cups).

2 Melt 2 tablespoons of the butter in a wide frying pan over medium heat. Add leeks and cook, stirring, until soft (8 to 10 minutes). Remove from heat and stir in thyme and lemon juice; season to taste with salt and white pepper.

3 Rinse fish and pat dry. Spread open and place, skin sides down, in a single layer in a greased baking pan. Spoon leek mixture down center of each fish. Melt remaining 2 tablespoons butter and drizzle over fish. Bake in a 400° oven until just opaque but still moist in thickest part; cut to test (8 to 10 minutes). Garnish with lemon wedges, if desired.

makes 6 servings

per serving: 341 calories, 35 g protein, 7 g carbohydrates, 19 g total fat, 114 mg cholesterol, 164 mg sodium

barbequed oysters

preparation time: about 25 minutes

¼ cup tomato-based chili sauce

1 tablespoon oyster or soy sauce

1 tablespoon lemon juice

2 teaspoons minced fresh cilantro

16 oysters in shells (about 4 in. long), scrubbed

1 In a small bowl, mix chili sauce, oyster sauce, lemon juice, and cilantro. To shuck each oyster, place shell, cupped side down, on a heavy towel. Grip curved end of shell with a towel and hold oyster level. Firmly insert an oyster knife into hinge at narrow end of oyster between top and bottom shell; twist to open. Slide oyster knife along underside of top shell to cut adductor muscle and free oyster. Remove top shell. Slide knife under oyster to cut free. Leave in shell and set shell side down on a tray.

2 Spoon an equal portion of the chili sauce mixture onto each oyster. Have barbecue ready with direct heat at hot. Set oysters in shells on grill and cook until juices bubble, about 4 minutes. Serve hot oysters in shells.

makes 8 appetizer servings

per serving: 93 calories, 9.9 g protein, 7.6 g carbohydrates, 2.3 g total fat, 55 mg cholesterol, 310 mg sodium

baked fish with tapenade & tomatoes

preparation time: 20 to 25 minutes

4 skinless white-fleshed fish fillets, such as sea bass or cod (about 6 oz. *each*), each ½ to ¾ inch thick

5 tablespoons olive oil or salad oil

2 medium-size tomatoes, cut into ½-inch-thick slices

1 can (6 oz.) pitted ripe olives, drained

1 clove garlic

1 Rinse fish, pat dry, and place in a single layer in a shallow baking pan. Brush with 1 tablespoon of the oil; top evenly with tomatoes. Bake in a 400° oven until fish is just opaque but still moist in thickest part; cut to test (10 to 15 minutes).

2 Meanwhile, in a food processor or blender, whirl olives and garlic until finely minced. Add remaining ¼ cup oil in a thin, steady stream, whirling until mixture forms a paste.

3 To serve, top fish evenly with olive mixture.

makes 4 servings

per serving: 398 calories, 36 g protein, 6 g carbohydrates, 25 g total fat, 54 mg cholesterol, 468 mg sodium

trout with carrot sambal

preparation time: 25 to 30 minutes

Carrot Sambal (recipe follows)

4 trout (about ½ lb. *each*)

Salt

2 tablespoons butter or margarine, melted

Lime wedges

1 Prepare Carrot Sambal; set aside.

2 If desired, cut off and discard trout heads. Rinse trout and pat dry. Sprinkle lightly with salt, brush with butter, and place on rack of a 12- by 14-inch broiler pan. Broil about 4 inches below heat, turning once, until fish is just opaque but still moist in thickest part; cut to test (8 to 10 minutes). Serve with Carrot Sambal; offer lime wedges.

CARROT SAMBAL

Place ⅓ cup unsweetened flaked coconut in a small bowl; add hot water to cover. Let stand until coconut is soft (about 10 minutes); drain well. Add 1 cup shredded carrots; 2 to 3 teaspoons minced fresh hot chile; 2 teaspoons minced fresh ginger; ½ teaspoon each ground coriander and crushed cumin seeds; and ¼ to ⅓ cup lime juice. Season to taste with salt.

makes 4 servings

per serving: 278 calories, 24 g protein, 9 g carbohydrates, 17 g total fat, 80 mg cholesterol, 132 mg sodium

BROILED TROUT DIJONNAISE

1 Follow directions above but omit Carrot Sambal.

2 To melted butter, add 1 tablespoon *each* dry white wine and Dijon mustard and ¼ teaspoon dry tarragon. Brush fish inside and out with about half the mixture. Broil as directed, brushing with remaining butter mixture after turning. Omit lime wedges; serve with lemon wedges.

makes 4 servings

per serving: 220 calories, 23 g protein, 0.6 g carbohydrates, 13 g total fat, 80 mg cholesterol, 229 mg sodium

ahi with bacon

preparation time: about 20 minutes

4 slices bacon

4 ahi (yellowfin tuna) steaks (about 1½ lbs. *total*),
   each about 1 inch thick

4 teaspoons butter or margarine

2 tablespoons soy sauce

½ cup dry white wine

TESTING FISH FOR DONENESS **Recognizing when fish is done is essential to cooking it well—if overcooked, it rapidly loses flavor and moisture. Most recipes in this book tell you to cook fish until it's "just opaque but still moist in thickest part." To test, cut to the center of the thickest portion of the whole fish, steak, or fillet— thinner parts may appear to be done while thicker portions are still cooking and uncooked inside. As a rule of thumb, allow 8 to 10 minutes of cooking time for each inch of thickness for fish cooked by any method other than microwaving.**

1 In a wide frying pan, cook bacon over medium-high heat until crisp (about 7 minutes). Lift out and drain. Discard all but 1 tablespoon of the drippings from pan.

2 Rinse fish and pat dry. Add to pan, increase heat to high, and cook, turning once, until browned. Dot fish with butter; add soy sauce and wine. Reduce heat to medium, cover, and cook until pale pink in center when cut (about 5 minutes). Transfer to warm plates; keep warm.

3 Boil sauce, uncovered, until reduced to about 3 tablespoons (2 to 3 minutes). Top each steak with sauce and 1 slice of the bacon.

makes 4 servings

per serving: 283 calories, 42 g protein, 1 g carbohydrates, 11 g total fat, 95 mg cholesterol, 735 mg sodium

oysters calico

preparation time: about 35 minutes

8 slices bacon

1 medium-size green bell pepper,
   stemmed, seeded, and chopped

1 medium-size onion, chopped

2 pounds shucked oysters, drained

1 cup shredded Cheddar cheese

1 In a wide frying pan, cook bacon over medium-high heat until crisp (about 7 minutes). Lift out, drain, and crumble; set aside. Discard all but 2 tablespoons of the drippings from pan.

2 Add bell pepper and onion to pan. Cook, stirring occasionally, until vegetables are soft (about 7 minutes). Set aside.

3 Rinse oysters in a colander and pat dry. Arrange snugly in a single layer in a shallow ovenproof serving dish. Broil about 4 inches below heat until edges of oysters begin to curl; turn over and broil until edges curl again (about 6 minutes total).

4 Evenly spoon onion mixture over oysters; sprinkle with bacon and cheese. Return to broiler and broil just until cheese is melted (1 to 2 minutes).

makes 4 to 6 servings

per serving: 237 calories, 18 g protein, 8 g carbohydrates, 14 g total fat, 110 mg cholesterol, 422 mg sodium

french tomato tart with anchovies

preparation time: about 1 hour

1½ cups all-purpose flour

½ cup butter or margarine

1 large egg

4 firm-ripe tomatoes, rinsed and cored

2 tablespoons Dijon mustard

2 cups shredded Swiss cheese

3 tablespoons olive oil

3 tablespoons tomato paste

3 tablespoons chopped shallots

1 clove garlic, peeled and minced

2 teaspoons fresh thyme leaves or dried thyme

2 teaspoons chopped fresh marjoram leaves
   or 1 teaspoon dried marjoram

1 teaspoon chopped fresh oregano leaves
   or ½ teaspoon dried oregano

6 to 8 canned anchovy fillets, drained

6 to 8 niçoise or calamata olives, pitted

Salt and pepper

Note: Up to 1 day ahead, bake crust, cool, wrap airtight, and keep at room temperature.

1 In a food processor or bowl, combine flour and butter. Whirl or rub with your fingers until fine crumbs form. Add egg and whirl or stir with a fork until dough holds together. Pat dough into a ball, then press evenly over bottom and sides of a 10-inch tart pan with removable rim.

2 Bake in a 325° oven until crust is pale gold, about 30 minutes (about 25 minutes in a convection oven). Meanwhile, cut tomatoes in half and gently squeeze out seeds. Cut tomatoes crosswise into 1-inch-thick slices, and lay on towels to drain. Save ends.

3 Remove baked crust from oven and turn oven to 400°. Spread mustard over bottom of crust, then sprinkle evenly with 1½ cups cheese. Fit largest tomato slices snugly in a single layer on cheese. Cut remaining tomato slices into pieces to fill the gaps; reserve extra tomato pieces for other uses.

4 In a small bowl, mix oil to blend with tomato paste, shallots, garlic, thyme, marjoram, and oregano. Spread over tomatoes. Sprinkle with remaining cheese. Arrange anchovies and olives on tomatoes.

5 Bake in a 400° oven until cheese is lightly browned, about 25 minutes (about 18 minutes in a convection oven). Remove pan rim. Cut the tart into wedges and serve hot or warm. Add salt and pepper to taste.

makes 6 or 7 servings

per serving: 441 calories, 15 g protein, 28 g carbohydrates, 30 g total fat, 98 mg cholesterol, 531 mg sodium

lemony fish with asparagus

preparation time: about 15 minutes

1 pound asparagus

2 teaspoons *each* **cornstarch, lemon juice, and salad oil**

¾ pound orange roughy, sea bass, or halibut fillets, *each* **about ½ inch thick, cut into 1- by 3-inch strips**

3 tablespoons salad oil

1 large clove garlic, minced or pressed

2 tablespoons regular-strength chicken broth or water

2 tablespoons lemon juice

1 Snap off and discard tough ends of asparagus; cut spears into ½-inch slanting slices. Set aside.

2 In a bowl, stir together cornstarch, the 2 teaspoons lemon juice, and the 2 teaspoons oil. Add fish and stir gently until evenly coated.

3 Place a wok over medium-high heat; when wok is hot, add 2 tablespoons of the oil. When oil is hot, add fish and stir-fry until opaque (about 2 minutes); remove fish from wok and set aside.

4 Pour remaining 1 tablespoon oil into wok. When oil begins to heat, add garlic and stir-fry for about 30 seconds. Then add asparagus and stir-fry for 1 minute. Stir together broth and the 2 tablespoons lemon juice; pour into wok, cover, and cook, stirring often, until asparagus is tender-crisp to bite (2 to 3 more minutes). Return fish and any accumulated juices to wok and stir just until heated through.

LEMONY FISH WITH FENNEL

Follow directions for Lemony Fish with Asparagus, but substitute 1 large fennel bulb for asparagus. To prepare fennel, trim off and discard stalks, reserving a few of the feathery leaves for garnish. Cut away and discard base; cut bulb in half lengthwise, then thinly slice crosswise. (Fennel may need to cook for a few more minutes than asparagus.) Garnish dish with reserved fennel leaves.

makes 3 or 4 servings

per serving: 199 calories, 16 g protein, 4 g carbohydrates, 13 g total fat, 40 mg cholesterol, 294 mg sodium

broiled fish dijon

preparation time: about 15 minutes

4 firm-textured white-fleshed fish fillets, such as sea bass or rockfish (6 to 8 oz. *each***), each ¾ to 1 inch thick**

4 teaspoons lemon juice

3 tablespoons Dijon mustard

1 clove garlic, minced or pressed

Paprika

2 tablespoons drained capers

1 Rinse fish, pat dry, and arrange in a single layer in a rimmed 10- by 15-inch baking pan or broiler pan. Drizzle with lemon juice.

2 In a small bowl, stir together mustard and garlic; spread over tops of fillets. Broil 4 to 6 inches below heat until fish is just opaque but still moist in thickest part; cut to test (8 to 10 minutes; if necessary, rotate pan to cook fish evenly).

3 Sprinkle fish with paprika and capers. Serve hot. Or, to serve cold, let cool; then cover and refrigerate for at least 30 minutes or up to 2 hours.

makes 4 servings

per serving: 208 calories, 37 g protein, 2 g carbohydrates, 5 g total fat, 81 mg cholesterol, 583 mg sodium

cambodian steamed mussels

preparation time: about 40 minutes

4 pounds mussels (beards pulled off), scrubbed

½ teaspoon salad oil

1 to 2 tablespoons minced fresh jalapeño chiles

3 cups fat-skimmed chicken broth

1 can (14 oz.) reduced-fat coconut milk

1 teaspoon ground dried turmeric

1 tablespoon rice vinegar

**1 cup pineapple chunks
(about ½ in.; fresh or canned)**

2 tablespoons chopped fresh cilantro

Salt

1 loaf (1 lb.) French bread, sliced

1 Discard any gaping mussels that do not close when the shells are tapped. In a 6- to 8-quart pan over high heat, stir oil and chiles until chiles are limp, 1 to 2 minutes.

2 Add chicken broth, canned coconut milk, ground turmeric, and rice vinegar. Bring mixture to a boil. Add mussels, cover, and cook until shells open, 6 to 10 minutes.

3 Ladle the mussels and broth into wide bowls. Spoon pineapple chunks equally over mussels and sprinkle portions with cilantro. Season to taste with salt. Serve mussels with bread to dip into the broth as you eat.

makes 4 servings

per serving: 540 calories, 32 g protein, 73 g carbohydrates, 12 g total fat, 37 mg cholesterol 1,151 mg sodium

sweet & sour fish

preparation time: about 30 minutes

Sweet-Sour Sauce (recipe follows)

About ⅓ cup cornstarch

**2 pounds turbot or halibut fillets,
cut into ½-inch squares**

About 6 tablespoons salad oil

1 clove garlic, minced or pressed

1 onion, cut into 1-inch cubes

**1 medium-size green bell pepper,
seeded and cut into ½-inch thick strips**

1 medium-size tomato, cut into 1-inch cubes

Fresh cilantro or Italian parsley (optional)

1 Prepare Sweet-Sour Sauce and set aside. Place cornstarch in a bag, add fish pieces, and shake to coat completely; shake off excess.

2 Place a wok over medium-high heat; when wok is hot, add 2 tablespoons of the oil. When oil is hot, add some of the fish; stir-fry until fish is browned on all sides and flakes when prodded (about 2 minutes). Remove from wok and keep warm. Repeat to cook remaining fish, adding about 2 tablespoons more oil.

3 Increase heat to high and pour 2 tablespoons more oil into wok. When oil is hot, add garlic, onion, and bell pepper; stir-fry for 2 minutes. Stir Sweet-Sour Sauce; pour into wok and stir in tomato. Bring to a boil, stirring. Return fish and any accumulated juices to wok; stir to combine. Garnish with cilantro, if desired.

SWEET-SOUR SAUCE

Stir together 1 tablespoon cornstarch and ¼ cup sugar. Stir in 2 tablespoons *each* soy sauce and catsup, ¼ cup distilled white vinegar, and ½ cup regular-strength chicken broth.

makes 4 servings

per serving: 736 calories, 35 g protein, 31 g carbohydrates, 52 g total fat, 104 mg cholesterol, 915 mg sodium

lime & chile monkfish with corn

preparation time: about 20 minutes

Lime-Chile Sauce (recipe follows)

1½ pounds monkfish fillets

3 tablespoons salad oil

1 cup fresh corn cut from cob or 1 cup frozen whole-kernel corn, thawed and drained

2 tablespoons chopped fresh cilantro

1 Prepare Lime-Chile Sauce; set aside.

2 Remove and discard membrane from fish. Rinse fish and pat dry, then cut into 1-inch chunks. Place a wok over high heat; when wok is hot, add 2 tablespoons of the oil. When oil is hot, add half the fish; stir-fry until fish flakes when prodded (about 2 minutes). Remove from wok and set aside. Repeat to cook remaining fish, adding remaining 1 tablespoon oil.

3 Pour Lime-Chile Sauce into wok and bring to a boil, stirring constantly. Add corn and stir until heated through (2 to 3 minutes). Return fish and any accumulated juices to wok; mix gently to heat. Pour onto a warm platter and sprinkle with cilantro.

LIME-CHILE SAUCE

Stir together ⅓ cup lime juice; 3 tablespoons regular-strength chicken broth; 1 clove garlic, minced or pressed; 1 small fresh Fresno or jalapeño chile, minced; ½ teaspoon each ground cumin, pepper, and sugar; and 1 teaspoon cornstarch.

makes 4 servings

per serving: 268 calories, 26 g protein, 11 g carbohydrates, 13 g total fat, 43 mg cholesterol, 88 mg sodium

TERIYAKI MONKFISH

Follow directions for Lime & Chile Monkfish with Corn, but omit Lime-Chile Sauce. Instead, use this teriyaki sauce: stir together ¼ cup regular-strength chicken or beef broth, 2 tablespoons *each* dry sherry and soy sauce, 2 teaspoons sugar, and 1 teaspoon cornstarch. Also omit corn; instead, use 1 cup cooked fresh shelled peas or 1 cup frozen peas, thawed and drained.

sautéed oysters with basil

preparation time: about 15 minutes

½ pound shucked fresh oysters, drained

All-purpose flour

2 tablespoons butter or margarine

1 tablespoon chopped fresh basil or ½ teaspoon dry basil

2 tablespoons dry white wine

1 Cut any large oysters into bite-size pieces. Pat oysters dry with paper towels; dredge in flour and shake off excess. Place a wok over medium-high heat; when wok is hot, add butter. When butter is melted, add oysters and sprinkle with basil. Stir-fry until oysters are golden brown (about 3 minutes), then transfer to a serving dish.

2 Add wine to wok and cook until sauce is reduced to 1 tablespoon. Spoon sauce over oysters.

makes 2 servings

per serving: 209 calories, 9 g protein, 11 g carbohydrates, 14 g total fat, 115 mg cholesterol, 201 mg sodium

squid & pea stir-fry

preparation time: about 35 minutes

Pan-fried Noodles (recipe follows)

1 pound squid

2 tablespoons salad oil

½ teaspoon minced fresh ginger

1 cup shelled peas (about I lb. unshelled)

½ cup regular-strength chicken broth

1 teaspoon soy sauce

1 tablespoon oyster sauce

¼ teaspoon sugar

2 teaspoons cornstarch and 1 tablespoon water, stirred together

1 Prepare Pan-fried Noodles and keep warm.

2 To clean each squid, gently pull on body to separate it from hood. Then pull out and discard long, clear quill from hood. Scoop out and discard contents of hood; rinse out hood. Set aside.

3 With a sharp knife, sever body between eyes and tentacles. Discard eyes and attached material. Pop out and discard hard black beak in center of tentacles. Rinse and drain tentacles; pat dry and set aside.

4 Pull off and discard thin, speckled membrane from hood; rinse and drain hood. Slit hood lengthwise and open flat. Make ½-inch-wide diagonal cuts across inside of hood. Repeat in opposite direction. Cut scored hood in about 2-inch-square pieces.

5 Place a wok over medium-high heat; when wok is hot, add 1 table-spoon of the oil. When oil begins to heat, add ginger; stir once. Add squid; stir-fry until edges curl (1 ½ to 2 minutes). Remove from wok.

6 Pour remaining 1 tablespoon oil into wok. When oil is hot, add peas and stir-fry for 1 minute. Add broth, soy, oyster sauce, and sugar; bring to a boil and boil for 1 minute. Stir cornstarch-water mixture; pour into wok and stir until sauce boils and thickens. Return squid to wok, stir, and serve at once, over Pan-fried Noodles.

PAN-FRIED NOODLES

Heat 2 tablespoons salad oil in a frying pan over medium-high heat. Spread 8 ounces Chinese wheat flour noodles, cooked and drained, in pan in a layer 1 inch thick. Cook until brown on bottom. Turn noodles over in 1 piece; add 1 tablespoon more salad oil and cook until browned on other side. Serve whole or in wedges.

makes 3 or 4 servings

per serving: 473 calories, 27g protein, 49 g carbohydrates, 19 g total fat, 49 mg cholesterol, 458 mg sodium

crab with emerald sauce

preparation time: about 30 minutes

8 ounces basil sprigs

4 ounces cilantro sprigs

8 ounces dried capellini

¼ cup seasoned rice vinegar; or ¼ cup rice vinegar and 1 teaspoon sugar

1 tablespoon minced lemon peel

1 tablespoon Asian sesame oil

¾ cup fat-free reduced-sodium chicken broth

2 tablespoons vegetable oil

⅓ to ½ pound cooked crabmeat

1 Reserve 4 of the basil sprigs and cilantro sprigs for garnish. Bring 8 cups water to a boil in a 4- to 5-quart pan over medium-high heat. Gather half the remaining fresh basil into a bunch. Holding stem ends with tongs, dip leaves into boiling water just until bright green (about 3 seconds). At once plunge into ice water. Repeat with cilantro and remaining basil.

2 Stir pasta into water and cook just until tender to bite (about 4 minutes); or cook according to package directions. Drain well. Place in a bowl. Add vinegar, lemon peel, and sesame oil; lift with 2 forks to mix. Keep warm.

3 Drain basil and cilantro; blot dry. Cut leaves from stems, discarding stems. Place leaves in a blender or food processor with broth and veg-etable oil. Whirl until smooth. Spread on individual plates. Top with pasta and crab. Garnish with reserved basil and cilantro sprigs.

makes 4 servings

per serving: 382 calories, 19 g protein, 49 g carbohydrates, 13 g total fat, 43 mg cholesterol, 485 mg sodium

oven-poached lingcod

preparation time: about 45 minutes

2 medium-size onions, sliced

12 whole black peppercorns

4 whole allspice

⅓ cup lemon juice

2 dry bay leaves

1 cup dry white wine

8 cups water

3 large leeks

1 tablespoon olive oil

2 pounds lingcod fillets (about 1 inch thick)

Salt and pepper (optional)

1 In a 4- to 5-quart pan, combine onions, peppercorns, allspice, lemon juice, bay leaves, wine, and water. Bring to a boil over high heat; then reduce heat, cover, and simmer for 20 minutes. Pour liquid through a fine strainer; discard residue and return liquid to pan.

2 While poaching liquid is simmering, trim ends and all but 3 inches of green tops from leeks; remove tough outer leaves. Split leeks lengthwise; rinse well, then thinly slice crosswise. Heat oil in a wide frying pan over medium heat; add leeks and cook, stirring occasionally, until soft (about 10 minutes). Remove from heat.

3 Rinse fish, pat dry, and place in a single layer in an oiled 9- by 13-inch baking dish. Bring strained poaching liquid to a boil and pour over fish (liquid should just cover fish; if necessary, add equal parts of hot water and wine to cover fish). Cover and bake in a 425° oven until fish is just opaque but still moist in thickest part; cut to test (about 6 minutes).

4 Lift fish from baking dish, drain well, place in a serving dish, and keep warm. Measure ½ cup of the poaching liquid and add to leeks. Bring to a boil, stirring; season to taste with salt and pepper, if desired. Pour sauce over fish.

makes 6 servings

per serving: 236 calories, 28 g protein, 15 g carbohydrates, 4 g total fat, 79 mg cholesterol, 708 mg sodium

crab cakes

preparation time: 45 to 50 minutes

2 pink or ruby grapefruit

¾ pound shelled cooked crab

2 tablespoons diced red bell pepper

1 tablespoon diced celery

1 tablespoon diced red onion

2 tablespoons chopped parsley

1 large egg

½ teaspoon dry mustard

¼ cup mayonnaise

⅛ teaspoon fresh-ground pepper

⅛ teaspoon cayenne

About 1 cup panko (Japanese-style coarse bread crumbs) or dried bread crumbs

6 to 7 tablespoons butter or margarine

Pink grapefruit sauce (recipe follows)

2 tablespoons minced parsley

1 With a knife, cut and discard peel and white membrane from grapefruit. Holding fruit over a strainer nested in a bowl, cut between inner membrane and segments to release; drop segments into strainer and collect juice to use for sauce. Discard membrane. Sort through crab and discard any bits of shell.

2 In another bowl, combine red bell pepper, celery, onion, chopped parsley, egg, mustard, mayonnaise, pepper, and cayenne. Mix well with a fork. Add crab and stir just to mix. Put panko in a shallow pan. Mound ⅛ of the crab mixture on panko, and pat crumbs lightly on top. With a spatula, transfer cake (it's fragile) to a sheet of waxed paper. Repeat with remaining crab mixture to shape and coat remaining cakes. Set slightly apart on waxed paper.

3 In a 10- to 12-inch non-stick frying pan over medium heat, melt 2 tablespoons butter. When hot, set crab cakes slightly apart in pan. Cook, turning once, until browned on both sides, 5 to 8 minutes total. Add more butter if needed to brown evenly. As cooked, set cakes on warm plates and keep warm.

4 Set pan with pink grapefruit sauce over high heat, add 4 tablespoons butter, in chunks, and stir until melted, about 1½ minutes. Spoon warm sauce equally around crab cakes. Garnish with grapefruit segments and sprinkle with parsley.

PINK GRAPEFRUIT SAUCE

In a 10- to 12-inch frying pan, combine 1 tablespoon butter or margarine, 1 tablespoon minced onion, and ¼ cup minced mushrooms. Stir often over high heat until mushrooms begin to brown, 2 to 3 minutes. Add ¼ teaspoon dried thyme, ½ cup dry white wine, and 2 cups pink or ruby grapefruit juice (include reserved juice from crab cakes, preceding). Boil over high heat, stirring occasionally, until mixture is reduced to ½ cup, about 15 minutes.

makes 8 first-course servings

per serving: 264 calories, 11 g protein, 16 g carbohydrates, 17 g total fat, 100 mg cholesterol, 293 mg sodium

crab in black bean sauce

preparation time: about 20 minutes

**1 large cooked crab in shell (1½ to 2 lbs.),
cleaned and cracked**

2 tablespoons salad oil

**1½ tablespoons fermented salted black beans,
rinsed, drained, and finely chopped**

1 large clove garlic, minced or pressed

¾ teaspoon minced fresh ginger

**1 green bell pepper, seeded and cut into 1-inch
squares**

1 tablespoon *each* soy sauce and dry sherry

**2 green onions (including tops),
cut into 1-inch lengths**

⅓ cup regular-strength chicken broth

1 Cut crab body into quarters; leave legs and claws whole. Set aside. Place a wok over high heat; when wok is hot, add oil. When oil begins to heat, add black beans, garlic, and ginger and stir once. Add bell pepper and stir-fry for 1 minute. Add crab, soy, sherry, onions, and broth; stir until crab is heated through (about 3 minutes).

makes 2 servings

per serving: 328 calories, 22 g protein, 7 g carbohydrates, 24 g total fat, 114 mg cholesterol, 1,248 mg sodium

CRAB IN TOMATO-GARLIC SAUCE

Follow directions for Crab in Black Bean Sauce, but increase garlic to 3 cloves and omit black beans and ginger. Add 2 large tomatoes, peeled, seeded, and chopped, along with bell pepper. Omit soy, sherry, and broth; instead, use ½ cup dry white wine.

CRAB IN CREAM SAUCE

Follow directions for Crab in Black Bean Sauce, using 1 tablespoon minced shallots and 1 red bell pepper, seeded and cut into 1-inch squares, in place of the black beans, ginger, and green bell pepper. Substitute ¼ cup whipping cream, 2 tablespoons dry white wine, 1 teaspoon Dijon mustard, and 1 tablespoon chopped parsley for the soy, sherry, green onions and broth.

poached fish with horseradish sauce

preparation time: about 45 minutes

**1½ pounds skinless, boneless lingcod, halibut,
rockfish, or sole fillets or steaks (fillets no
thicker than 1 inch, steaks about 1 inch thick)**

**About ⅔ cup fat-free reduced-sodium chicken
broth**

1 tablespoon cornstarch

1 tablespoon prepared horseradish

**8 to 12 hot boiled tiny potatoes
(*each* about 1 inch in diameter)**

**3 green onions, cut into 2-inch lengths
and slivered**

1 Rinse fish and pat dry; fold any thin fillets in half. Arrange fish in a shallow 8-inch baking dish. Pour ⅔ cup of the broth over fish. Cover and bake in a 400° oven until fish is just opaque but still moist in thickest part; cut to test (about 15 minutes). With a slotted spatula, lift fish to a warm platter; keep warm.

2 Drain cooking liquid from baking dish into a measuring cup; you should have about 1 cup. If necessary, boil to reduce to 1 cup or add more broth to make 1 cup. In a 1 ½- to 2-quart pan, smoothly blend cornstarch, horseradish, and cooking liquid. Bring to a boil over high heat, stirring.

3 Spoon sauce evenly over fish. Arrange potatoes on platter around fish; sprinkle with onions.

makes 4 servings

per serving: 206 calories, 32 g protein, 13 g carbohydrates, 2 g total fat, 89 mg cholesterol, 218 mg sodium

salmon steaks with spinach

preparation time: about 40 minutes

¼ **cup butter or margarine**

1 **large onion, chopped**

1 **clove garlic, minced or pressed**

1½ **to 2 pounds spinach, stems removed, leaves rinsed**

Salt and pepper

4 **salmon steaks (***each* **about 1 inch thick)**

1 **teaspoon dry dill weed**

Lemon wedges

1 Melt 3 tablespoons of the butter in a 5- to 6-quart pan over medium heat. Add onion and garlic and cook, stirring occasionally, until onion is very soft (about 15 minutes).

2 Meanwhile, cut spinach leaves into 1-inch-wide strips.

3 Stir spinach (with water that clings to leaves) into onion mixture. Cover pan, increase heat to medium-high, and cook until spinach is wilted and bright green in color (2 to 4 minutes). Uncover and cook until liquid has evaporated, stirring occasionally. Remove from heat; season to taste with salt and pepper. Transfer to a warm rimmed platter and keep warm.

4 While spinach is cooking, rinse salmon and pat dry; then place in a lightly greased baking pan. Broil 4 inches below heat for 5 minutes. Turn salmon over; sprinkle with salt, pepper, and dill weed, then dot with remaining 1 tablespoon butter. Continue to broil until fish is just opaque but still moist in thickest part; cut to test (about 5 more minutes).

5 To grill salmon: Place steaks on a lightly greased range-top grill; cook for time specified in broiling instructions above, turning and seasoning with salt, pepper, dill, and butter after 5 minutes.

6 To serve, place salmon atop spinach and garnish with lemon wedges.

makes 4 servings

per serving: 430 calories, 44 g protein, 8 g carbohydrates, 25 g total fat, 140 mg cholesterol, 319 mg sodium

broiled salmon with sherry-soy butter

preparation time: 20 to 25 minute

1 **tablespoon sesame seeds**

2 **tablespoons butter or margarine**

2 **tablespoons** *each* **thinly sliced green onion (including top) and dry sherry**

1 **tablespoon soy sauce**

4 **boned baby salmon (about** ½ **lb.** *each***), heads removed; or 4 salmon fillets or steaks (about 6 oz.** *each***)**

1 Toast sesame seeds in a small frying pan over medium heat until golden (3 to 5 minutes), shaking pan often. Add butter, onion, sherry, and soy sauce; cook, stirring, until butter is melted. Remove from heat.

2 Rinse fish and pat dry. Place on greased rack of a large broiler pan (spread baby salmon open and place skin sides down). Brush with butter mixture. Broil about 4 inches below heat until just opaque but still moist in thickest part; cut to test (6 to 8 minutes). Serve with any remaining butter mixture.

makes 4 servings

per serving: 320 calories, 34 g protein, 2 g carbohydrates, 18 g total fat, 109 mg cholesterol, 392 mg sodium

mango-shrimp tostadas

preparation time: about 35 minutes

1 firm-ripe mango

1 firm-ripe avocado

6 tablespoons lime juice

¾ pound (26 to 30 per lb.) shelled, deveined cooked shrimp, rinsed and drained

1 teaspoon minced fresh serrano chili

⅓ cup chopped green onions

4 flour tortillas

1 can (16 oz.) low-fat refried black beans

¼ cup fat-skimmed chicken broth

3 cups shredded iceberg lettuce

½ cup nonfat sour cream

Salt

1 Cut pit and peel from mango and discard. Cut fruit into small pieces and put in a bowl.

2 Pit and peel avocado. Cut into small pieces and add to mango. Add lime juice, shrimp, chili, and green onions; mix gently.

3 Place tortillas side by side on a 14- by 17-inch baking sheet. Bake in a 400° oven until crisp and lightly browned, about 10 minutes (about 9 minutes in a convection oven), turning tortillas over once after 4 to 5 minutes. Let cool on pan 1 to 2 minutes.

4 Meanwhile, combine refried beans and broth in a microwave-safe bowl, cover, and heat in a microwave oven on full power (100%) until hot, about 1 minute.

5 Place tortillas on plates. Spread beans equally onto tortillas. Scatter lettuce equally over beans, then top lettuce with shrimp mixture and sour cream. Add salt to taste.

makes 4 servings

per serving: 423 calories, 29 g protein, 53 g carbohydrates, 12 g total fat, 166 mg cholesterol, 784 mg sodium

snapper florentine

preparation time: about 25 minutes

¾ cup sour cream

⅓ cup mayonnaise

2 tablespoons *each* all-purpose flour and lemon juice

¼ teaspoon dry dill weed

1 pound Pacific or red snapper fillets (*each* about ½ inch thick)

Salt and pepper

1½ to 2 pounds spinach, stems removed, leaves rinsed

Paprika

1 In a bowl, whisk sour cream, mayonnaise, flour, lemon juice, and dill weed until smoothly blended; set aside.

2 Rinse fish, pat dry, and arrange in a single layer in a 9- by 13-inch baking dish. Season to taste with salt and pepper, then spread evenly with sour cream mixture. Bake in a 400° oven until fish is just opaque but still moist in thickest part; cut to test (7 to 10 minutes).

3 Meanwhile, place spinach (with water that clings to leaves) in a wide frying pan. Cover and cook over medium-high heat, stirring occasionally, until wilted and bright green in color (2 to 4 minutes); drain well. Arrange spinach on a warm platter; top with fish. Spoon any sauce remaining in baking dish over fish; sprinkle with paprika.

makes 4 servings

per serving: 379 calories, 29 g protein, 10 g carbohydrates, 25 g total fat, 72 mg cholesterol, 298 mg sodium

malaysian hot shrimp

preparation time: 40 minutes

3 small dried hot red chiles, seeded

1½ tablespoons tamarind paste;
   or 1½ tablespoons cider vinegar
   and ¼ teaspoon sugar

1 teaspoon shrimp paste or sauce;
   or anchovy paste

¼ cup tomato paste

2 tablespoons salad oil

2 tablespoons minced shallots

2 cloves garlic, minced or pressed

1 small onion, thinly sliced

1 pound jumbo raw shrimp (16 to 20 per lb.),
   shelled and deveined

Fresh cilantro sprigs

1 Cover chiles with hot water and let stand until soft (about 10 minutes). In a small bowl, combine tamarind paste and ¼ cup water; with your hands, separate seeds from paste. (Or mix vinegar and sugar with 3 tablespoons water.)

2 Press tamarind mixture through a wire strainer into a blender or food processor; discard solids remaining in strainer. (Or pour vinegar mixture into blender.)

3 Drain chiles and add to blender with shrimp paste, tomato paste, and 2 tablespoons water; whirl until puréed. Set aside.

4 Heat oil in a wide frying pan or wok over medium-high heat. Add shallots, garlic, and onion; cook, stirring, until onion is soft (2 to 3 minutes). Stir in tamarind mixture and cook, stirring, until mixture boils.

5 Reduce heat to medium and add shrimp; cook, stirring often, just until shrimp are opaque in thickest part when cut (4 to 5 minutes). Garnish with cilantro.

makes 3 or 4 servings

per serving: 196 calories, 21 g protein, 8 g carbohydrates, 9 g total fat, 131 mg cholesterol, 336 mg sodium

steamed soft-shell crab with ginger sauce

preparation time: about 25 minutes

6 cleaned soft-shell blue crabs
   (about 2 oz. *each*), thawed if frozen

⅓ cup rice wine vinegar

1 to 2 tablespoons sliced green onion
   (including top)

1½ tablespoons minced fresh ginger

1 teaspoon sugar

1 Place a steamer rack over 1 to 2 inches boiling water in a large pan or wok. Lay crabs, back sides up, in a single layer on rack. Cover and steam over high heat until crabs are opaque in center of body when cut (about 8 minutes).

2 Meanwhile, stir together vinegar, onion, ginger, and sugar in a small bowl.

3 Transfer crabs to warm plates. Offer ginger sauce to spoon over each portion.

makes 2 or 3 servings

per serving: 122 calories, 22 g protein, 3 g carbohydrates, 2 g total fat, 108 mg cholesterol, 305 mg sodium

steamed clams with linguiça & pasta

preparation time: about 35 minutes

⅓ **pound linguiça sausage, cut into ¼-inch-thick slices**

1 medium-size onion, chopped

1 large red bell pepper, seeded and diced

3 cups water

1 ½ cups regular-strength chicken broth

¾ cup dry white wine

¼ cup rice-shaped or other tiny pasta

½ teaspoon dry basil

32 to 36 clams suitable for steaming, scrubbed

Minced parsley

1 In a 5- to 6-quart pan, cook sausage over medium-high heat, stirring, until lightly browned. Add onion and bell pepper; cook, stirring, until onion is soft (about 10 minutes). Add water, broth, wine, pasta, and basil. Bring to a boil; reduce heat, cover, and simmer until pasta is al dente (8 to 10 minutes).

2 Skim and discard fat from broth. Add clams. Cover and bring to a boil; reduce heat and simmer until clams open (5 to 7 minutes). Lift out clams and distribute equally among 4 wide, shallow bowls. Ladle broth over clams. Lightly sprinkle each serving with parsley.

makes 4 servings

per serving: 253 calories, 17 g protein, 15 g carbohydrates, 13 g total fat, 52 mg cholesterol, 687 mg sodium

stir-fried shrimp with green onions

preparation time: about 20 minutes

1 pound large raw shrimp (25 to 30 per lb.), shelled and deveined

1 tablespoon rice wine or dry sherry

1 tablespoon cornstarch

2 tablespoons salad oil

4 green onions (including tops), thinly sliced

Soy sauce (optional)

1 In a small bowl, mix shrimp, wine, and cornstarch.

2 Heat oil in a wok or wide frying pan over high heat. Add shrimp mixture and cook, stirring, until shrimp turn bright pink (2 to 3 minutes). Add onions and continue to cook, stirring, until shrimp are just opaque in center; cut to test (about 2 more minutes). Offer soy sauce to add to taste, if desired.

makes 3 servings

per serving: 228 calories, 25 g protein, 5 g carbohydrates, 11 g total fat, 186 mg cholesterol, 183 mg sodium

clam paella for two

preparation time: about 45 minutes

1 tablespoon olive oil

1 clove garlic, minced or pressed

¼ teaspoon ground turmeric

⅔ cup long-grain white rice

2 tablespoons finely chopped parsley

8 ounces cherry tomatoes, cut into halves

⅔ cup dry white wine

¾ cup bottled clam juice or low-sodium
  chicken broth

24 small hard-shell clams in shell, scrubbed

1 Heat oil in a wide frying pan over medium heat. Add garlic, turmeric, and rice. Cook, stirring often, until rice begins to look opaque (about 3 minutes). Stir in parsley, tomatoes, wine, and clam juice. Brig to a boil; then reduce heat, cover, and simmer for 15 minutes.

2 Arrange clams over rice. Cover and continue to cook until clams pop open and rice is tender to bite (8 to 10 more minutes). Discard any unopened clams; then spoon clams and rice into bowls.

makes 2 servings

per serving: 452 calories, 29 g protein, 61 g carbohydrates, 9 g total fat, 61 mg cholesterol, 313 mg sodium

scallops with broccoli & bell pepper

preparation time: about 25 minutes

2 tablespoons reduced-sodium soy sauce

4 teaspoons cornstarch

¾ cup fat-free reduced-sodium chicken broth

2 tablespoons dry sherry

2 teaspoons finely minced fresh ginger

1½ teaspoons sugar

1 pound sea scallops

2 cups broccoli flowerets

1 medium-size red or green bell pepper,
  seeded and cut into thin strips

1 small onion, thinly sliced

2 teaspoons vegetable oil

1 or 2 cloves garlic, minced or pressed

1 To prepare sauce, in a small bowl, stir together soy sauce and cornstarch until blended. Stir in broth, sherry, ginger, and sugar; set aside.

2 Rinse scallops and pat dry; cut into bite-size pieces, if desired. Set aside.

3 In a wide nonstick frying pan or wok, combine broccoli, bell pepper, onion, and ⅓ cup water. Cover and cook over medium-high heat just until vegetables are tender to bite (about 4 minutes). Uncover and stir-fry until liquid has evaporated.

4 Stir sauce well and pour into pan. Cook, stirring, until sauce boils and thickens slightly (1 to 2 minutes). Transfer vegetable mixture to a serv-ing bowl and keep warm. Wipe pan clean.

5 Heat oil in pan over medium-high heat. When oil is hot, add garlic and 1 tablespoon water to pan. Stir-fry just until garlic is fragrant (about 30 seconds). Add scallops. Stir-fry until scallops are just opaque in center; cut to test (3 to 4 minutes). Pour scallops and any pan juices over vegetable mixture; mix gently but thoroughly.

makes 4 servings

per serving: 196 calories, 23 g protein, 17 g carbohydrates, 3 g total fat, 37 mg cholesterol, 591 mg sodium

lemony shrimp tostadas

preparation time: about 15 minutes
chilling time: at least 20 minutes

1 pound tiny cooked shrimp

1 cup peeled, minced jicama

3 tablespoons sliced green onions

1 teaspoon grated lemon peel

3 tablespoons lemon juice

2 teaspoons honey

White pepper

About 1 ½ cups salsa of your choice

6 crisp corn taco shells or warm tortillas

3 cups shredded lettuce

1 medium-size firm-ripe tomato, finely chopped

1 In a nonmetal bowl, mix shrimp, jicama, onions, lemon peel, lemon juice, and honey; season to taste with white pepper. Cover and refrigerate for at least 20 minutes or up to 3 hours.

2 To serve, place a taco shell on each of 6 dinner plates; top equally with lettuce. Scoop out shrimp mixture with a slotted spoon, drain, and divide equally among taco shells. Top equally with tomato. Add salsa to taste.

makes 6 servings

per serving: 156 calories, 18 g protein, 18 g carbohydrates, 2 g total fat, 148 mg cholesterol, 217 mg sodium

shrimp custard

preparation time: about 45 minutes

8 ounces small cooked shrimp

1 cup nonfat milk

1 large egg

2 large egg whites

4 teaspoons dry sherry

2 teaspoons finely chopped fresh ginger

2 teaspoons reduced-sodium soy sauce

1 clove garlic, minced or pressed

⅛ teaspoon Asian sesame oil

⅛ teaspoon ground white pepper

1 teaspoon sesame seeds

1 Divide half the shrimp evenly among four ¾-cup custard cups or oven-proof bowls; cover and refrigerate remaining shrimp. Set custard cups in a large baking pan at least 2 inches deep.

2 In a medium-size bowl, combine milk, egg, egg whites, sherry, ginger, soy sauce, garlic, oil, and white pepper; beat lightly just until blended. Pour egg mixture evenly over shrimp in custard cups.

3 Set pan on center rack of a 325° oven. Pour boiling water into pan around cups up to level of custard. Bake until custard jiggles only slightly in center when cups are gently shaken (about 25 minutes). Lift cups from pan. Let stand for about 5 minutes before serving. (At this point, you may let cool; then cover and refrigerate until next day and serve cold.)

4 Meanwhile, toast sesame seeds in a small frying pan over medium heat, stirring often, until golden (about 3 minutes). Remove from pan and set aside. Just before serving, top custards with remaining shrimp; then sprinkle with sesame seeds.

makes 4 servings

per serving: 120 calories, 18 g protein, 4 g carbohydrates, 2 g total fat, 165 mg cholesterol, 303 mg sodium

salmon sauté with citrus sauce

preparation time: about 40 minutes

3 or 4 medium-size oranges

1 large pink grapefruit

1 large lime

3 green onions

1 tablespoon butter or margarine

1 pound salmon fillets, skinned
    and cut into 1- by 2-inch strips

¼ cup dry vermouth

⅓ cup orange marmalade

1 tablespoon chopped fresh mint

Mint sprigs (optional)

Salt and pepper

1 Shred enough peel (colored part only) from oranges, grapefruit, and lime to make ½ teaspoon of each kind of peel. Combine peels in a small bowl; cover and set aside.

2 Cut off and discard remaining peel and all white membrane from grapefruit, lime, and 2 of the oranges. Holding fruit over a bowl to catch juice, cut between membranes to release segments; set segments aside. Pour juice from bowl into a glass measure. Squeeze juice from remaining oranges; add enough of this orange juice to juice in glass measure to make ½ cup (reserve remaining orange juice for other uses). Set juice aside.

3 Trim and discard ends of onions. Cut onions into 2-inch lengths, then cut each piece lengthwise into slivers; set aside.

4 Melt butter in a wide nonstick frying pan or wok over medium-high heat. Add fish. Stir-fry gently (flipping with a spatula, if needed) until fish is just opaque but still moist in thickest part; cut to test (about 4 minutes). With a slotted spoon, transfer fish to a large bowl; keep warm.

5 Add citrus juices and vermouth to pan. Bring to a boil; then boil, stirring often, until reduced to ⅓ cup (about 3 minutes). Reduce heat to low, add marmalade, and stir until melted. Add onions and citrus segments; stir gently just until heated through. Remove from heat and stir in chopped mint.

6 Spoon fruit sauce over fish; mix gently. Divide fish mixture among 4 individual rimmed plates; garnish with citrus peels and mint sprigs, if desired. Season to taste with salt and pepper.

makes 4 servings

per serving: 352 calories, 24 g protein, 39 g carbohydrates, 10 g total fat, 70 mg cholesterol, 98 mg sodium

tomato-caper sauce

preparation time: 25 minutes

1 teaspoon olive oil

1 medium-size onion, finely chopped

1 clove garlic, minced or pressed

1 can (about 14½ oz.) diced tomatoes

2 teaspoons drained capers

1 tablespoon lemon juice

2 tablespoons minced parsley

Heat oil in a wide nonstick frying pan over medium heat. Add onion and garlic; cook, stirring often, until onion is soft (about 5 minutes). Add tomatoes and capers. Bring to a gentle boil. Cook, uncovered, stirring often, until thickened (about 10 minutes). Stir in lemon juice and parsley. Serve over hot cooked fish.

makes about 2 cups

per tablespoon: 6 calories, 0.2 g protein, 19 carbohydrates, 0.2 g total fat, 0 mg cholesterol, 26 mg sodium

cajun scallops & brown rice

preparation time: about 55 minutes

4 1/2 cups low-sodium chicken broth

1 1/2 cups long-grain brown rice

1 1/2 pounds bay scallops

1 teaspoon paprika

1/2 teaspoon ground white pepper

1/4 teaspoon ground allspice

2 teaspoons salad oil

1 1/2 tablespoons cornstarch blended
with 1/3 cup cold water

1/2 cup reduced-fat sour cream

Parsley sprigs

1 In a 3- to 4-quart pan, bring 3½ cups of the broth to a boil over high heat. Add rice; reduce heat, cover, and simmer until rice is tender to bite (about 45 minutes).

2 About 10 minutes before rice is done, rinse scallops and pat dry; then mix with paprika, white pepper, and allspice. Heat oil in a wide nonstick frying pan over high heat. Add scallops and cook, turning often with a wide spatula, until just opaque in center; cut to test (2 to 3 minutes). With a slotted spoon, transfer scallops to a bowl.

3 Bring pan juices to a boil over high heat; boil, uncovered, until reduced to ¼ cup. Add remaining 1 cup broth and return to a boil. Stir in cornstarch mixture; bring to a boil, stirring. Stir in sour cream and scallops. Serve over rice; garnish with parsley sprigs.

makes 6 servings

per serving: 350 calories, 26 g protein, 43 g carbohydrates, 8 g total fat, 44 mg cholesterol, 226 mg sodium

stir-fried scallops & asparagus

preparation time: about 30 minutes

8 ounces bay or sea scallops

1/2 cup unseasoned rice vinegar
or white wine vinegar

2 tablespoons sugar

1 teaspoon *each* Asian sesame oil and
reduced-sodium soy sauce

2 tablespoons salad oil

1 pound asparagus, tough ends removed, stalks
cut into about 1/2-inch-thick slanting slices

3 tablespoons water

8 ounces dry vermicelli or spaghettini

1 clove garlic, minced or pressed

1 tablespoon minced fresh ginger

Lemon slices

1 Rinse scallops and pat dry. If using sea scallops, cut into ½-inch pieces. Set aside. In a small bowl, stir together vinegar, sugar, sesame oil, and soy sauce. Set aside.

2 Heat 1 tablespoon of the salad oil in a wok or wide frying pan over high heat. Add asparagus and stir to coat; then add the 3 tablespoons water. Cover and cook until asparagus is tender-crisp to bite (3 to 5 minutes). Lift asparagus from pan and keep warm. Set pan aside.

3 In a 5- to 6-quart pan, cook vermicelli in about 3 quarts boiling water until just tender to bite (8 to 10 minutes); or cook according to package directions. Drain well, pour into a large bowl, and keep warm.

4 Heat remaining 1 tablespoon salad oil in frying pan over high heat. Add garlic, ginger, and scallops. Cook, turning often with a wide spatula, until scallops are just opaque in center; cut to test (2 to 3 minutes).

5 Return asparagus to pan and add vinegar mixture; stir just until sugar is dissolved. Pour scallop mixture over pasta and mix gently. Garnish with lemon slices.

makes 4 servings

per serving: 375 calories, 19 g protein, 54 g carbohydrates, 9 g total fat, 19 mg cholesterol, 147 mg sodium

gingered chili shrimp

preparation time: about 45 minutes

1 cup long-grain white rice

1 tablespoon sugar

3 tablespoons catsup

1 tablespoon *each* cider vinegar and reduced-sodium soy sauce

1/2 to 1 teaspoon crushed red pepper flakes

1 tablespoon salad oil

1 pound large raw shrimp (31 to 35 per lb.), shelled (leave tails attached) and deveined

1 tablespoon minced fresh ginger

2 cloves garlic, minced or pressed

1/2 teaspoon Asian sesame oil

About 1/4 cup sliced green onions, or to taste

1 In a 3- to 4-quart pan, bring 2 cups water to a boil over high heat; stir in rice. Reduce heat, cover, and simmer until liquid has been absorbed and rice is tender to bite (about 20 minutes).

2 Meanwhile, in a small bowl, stir together sugar, catsup, vinegar, soy sauce, and red pepper flakes until sugar is dissolved; set aside.

3 Heat salad oil in a wide nonstick frying pan or wok over medium-high heat. When oil is hot, add shrimp. Stir-fry until just opaque in center; cut to test (3 to 4 minutes). Remove shrimp from pan with tongs or a slotted spoon; keep warm.

4 To pan, add ginger and garlic; stir-fry just until garlic is fragrant (about 30 seconds; do not scorch). Stir catsup mixture and pour into pan; bring to a boil, stirring. Remove pan from heat and add shrimp and sesame oil; mix gently but thoroughly.

5 Spoon rice onto a rimmed platter; spoon shrimp mixture over rice and sprinkle with onions.

makes 4 servings

per serving: 336 calories, 23 g protein, 46 g carbohydrates, 6 g total fat, 140 mg cholesterol, 423 mg sodium

fish with herbs

preparation time: about 40 minutes

2 pounds boneless, skinless striped bass or sole fillets

1/2 cup *each* dry white wine and low-sodium chicken broth

1/4 cup minced shallots

1 tablespoon chopped fresh tarragon, thyme, or sage

6 to 8 thin lemon slices

6 to 8 tarragon, thyme, or sage sprigs

2 teaspoons cornstarch blended with 1 tablespoon cold water

Salt and pepper

1 Rinse fish and pat dry. Then arrange fillets, overlapping slightly, in a 9- by 13-inch baking dish. Pour wine and broth over fish; sprinkle with shallots and chopped tarragon. Lay lemon slices and tarragon sprigs on fish. Bake in a 375° oven until fish is just opaque but still moist in thickest part; cut to test (about 15 minutes).

2 Keeping fish in dish, carefully spoon off pan juices into a small pan. Cover fish and keep warm. Bring pan juices to a boil over high heat; then boil, uncovered, until reduced to 3/4 cup (about 5 minutes). Stir in cornstarch mixture; bring to a boil, stirring. Season sauce to taste with salt and pepper, then pour over fish.

makes 6 servings

per serving: 178 calories, 27 g protein, 4 g carbohydrates, 4 g total fat, 121 mg cholesterol, 112 mg sodium

scallop & pea pod stir-fry with papaya

preparation time: about 25 minutes

2 teaspoons cornstarch

1 tablespoon honey

1 tablespoon lemon juice

1/2 teaspoon ground ginger

1/2 teaspoon Chinese five-spice (or 1/8 teaspoon *each* anise seeds, ground allspice, ground cinnamon, and ground cloves)

2 medium-size papayas

1 pound sea scallops

1 tablespoon butter or margarine

1 1/2 cups fresh Chinese pea pods (also called snow or sugar peas or sugar snap peas, ends and strings removed; or 1 package (about 6 oz.) frozen Chinese pea pods, thawed and drained

1 To prepare ginger sauce, in a small bowl, stir together cornstarch and 1/4 cup water until blended. Stir in honey, lemon juice, ginger, and five-spice; set aside.

2 Cut unpeeled papayas lengthwise into halves; remove and discard seeds. Set papaya halves, cut side up, on a platter; cover and set aside.

3 Rinse scallops and pat dry; cut into bite-size pieces, if desired. Melt butter in a wide nonstick frying pan or wok over medium-high heat. Add scallops and fresh pea pods (if using frozen pea pods, add later, as directed below). Stir-fry until scallops are just opaque in center; cut to test (3 to 4 minutes).

4 Stir ginger sauce well, then pour into pan. Stir in frozen pea pods, if using. Cook, stirring, until sauce boils and thickens slightly (1 to 2 minutes). Spoon scallop mixture equally into papaya halves.

makes 4 servings

per serving: 220 calories, 21 g protein, 26 g carbohydrates, 4 g total fat, 45 mg cholesterol, 219 mg sodium

salt-grilled shrimp

preparation time: 35 minutes

1 1/2 pounds extra-jumbo raw shrimp (16 to 20 per lb.)

About 2 tablespoons sea salt or kosher salt

5 to 6 ounces Belgian endive, separated into leaves, rinse, and crisped

8 ounces small romaine lettuce leaves, rinsed and crisped

12 ounces tiny red and/or yellow cherry tomatoes

About 1/2 cup balsamic vinegar

1 Insert a wooden pick under back of each shrimp between shell segments; gently pull up to remove vein. If vein breaks, repeat in another place. Rinse and drain deveined shrimp; then roll in salt to coat lightly.

2 Mix endive, lettuce, any tomatoes in a large bowl.

3 Place shrimp on a lightly greased grill 4 to 6 inches above a solid bed of hot coals. Cook, turning once, until shrimp are just opaque in center; cut to test (about 8 minutes). Meanwhile, divide salad among individual plates.

4 To serve, arrange shrimp atop salsas. To eat, shell shrimp any season to taste with vinegar, oil, and pepper.

makes 4 servings

per serving: 213 calories, 30 g protein, 9 g carbohydrates, 6 g total fat, 210 mg cholesterol, 1,326 mg sodium

shrimp with black bean sauce

preparation time: about 40 minutes

8 tablespoons fermented salted black beans, rinsed and drained

4 ounces lean ground pork

1 large red bell pepper, seeded and finely chopped

12 ounces mushrooms, thinly sliced

3 cloves garlic, minced or pressed

1 tablespoon minced fresh ginger

1 cup low-sodium chicken broth

2 tablespoons oyster sauce

2 tablespoon cornstarch

1 tablespoon salad oil

12 ounces shelled, deveined medium-size raw shrimp (about 36 per lb.)

6 green onions, thinly sliced

6 cups finely shredded papa cabbage

1 In a large bowl, mix beans, pork, bell pepper, mushrooms, garlic, and ginger. In a small bowl, stir together broth, oyster sauce, and cornstarch; set aside.

2 Heat oil in a wide nonstick frying pan over high heat. Add shrimp and cook, stirring, until just opaque in center; cut to test (2 to 3 minutes). Remove from pan and set aside.

3 Add pork-mushroom mixture to pan and cook, stirring often, until meat is lightly browned (about 5 minutes). Add broth mixture and bring to a boil, stirring. Mix in shrimp and onions. Arrange cabbage on a platter; tap with shrimp mixture.

makes 6 servings

per serving: 175 calories, 20 g protein, 12 g carbohydrates, 6 g total fat, 99 mg cholesterol, 576 mg sodium

steamed clams with garlic

preparation time: about 50 minutes

1 teaspoon butter or margarine

2 medium-size onions, thinly sliced

1/4 to 1/2 cup chopped garlic

1/4 cup water

2 medium-size tomatoes, chopped

1 teaspoon *each* paprika, dry thyme, and black pepper

1/8 teaspoon ground red pepper (cayenne)

1 cup dry white wine

36 small hard-shell clams in shell, scrubbed

1 Melt butter in a 5- to 6-quart pan over medium heat. Add onions, garlic, and water. Cook, stirring often, until liquid has evaporated and onions are soft (about 10 minutes).

2 Stir in tomatoes, paprika, thyme, black pepper, and red pepper; cook, uncovered, for 5 minutes. Add wine and bring to a boil over high heat.

3 Add clams; reduce heat, cover, and boil gently until shells pop open (about 10 minutes). Discard any unopened clams; then ladle clams and sauce into wide bowls.

makes 4 servings

per serving: 225 calories, 20 g protein, 21 g carbohydrates, 3 g total fat, 48 mg cholesterol, 102 mg sodium

cracked crab with onion

preparation time: about 25 minutes

1/3 cup dry sherry

1/3 cup water

1/4 cup oyster sauce

2 teaspoons cornstarch

14 green onions

1 tablespoon vegetable oil

3 tablespoons minced fresh ginger

3 cooked Dungeness crabs (about 6 lbs. *total*), cleaned and cracked

1 In a small bowl, stir together sherry, 1/3 cup water, oyster sauce, and cornstarch until blended; set aside. Cut onions into 2-inch lengths, keeping white and green parts separate.

2 Heat oil in a wide nonstick frying pan or wok over medium-high heat. Add ginger and white parts of onions; stir-fry until onions just begin to brown (about 2 minutes). Stir sherry mixture and pour into pan; stir until sauce boils and thickens slightly (about 1 minute). Add crab and green parts of onions; stir to coat with sauce. Reduce heat to low, cover, and cook, stirring occasionally, until crab is heated through (5 to 8 minutes).

makes 6 servings

per serving: 163 calories, 21 g protein, 8 g carbohydrates, 3 g total fat, 64 mg cholesterol, 805 mg sodium

grilled scallops with pear-ginger coulis

preparation time: about 35 minutes

4 teaspoons olive oil

1 small onion, chopped

2 tablespoons chopped fresh ginger

3 medium-size firm-ripe pears (1 1/4 to 1 1/2 lbs. total), peeled, cored, and diced

1/4 cup rice vinegar or white wine vinegar

1 pound sea scallops, rinsed and patted dry

1 Heat 1 tablespoon of the oil in a 2-quart pan over medium-high heat. Add onion and cook, stirring often, until soft but not browned (3 to 5 minutes). Add ginger, pears, and vinegar. Cook, stirring occasionally, until pears are tender when pierced (12 to 15 minutes). Transfer mixture to a food processor or blender; whirl until smoothly puréed. Return to pan and keep warm over lowest heat.

2 Meanwhile, cut scallops in half horizontally, if necessary, to make 1/2-inch-thick discs. Lightly mix scallops and remaining 1 teaspoon oil. Thread a fourth of the scallops on each of 4 metal skewers, piercing scallops horizontally (through diameter) so they lie flat.

3 Place skewers on a greased grill 4 to 6 inches above a solid bed of hot coals. Cook, turning once, until scallops are opaque in center; cut to test (5 to 7 minutes). Spoon the warm pear mixture onto 4 dinner plates; lay a skewer alongside.

makes 4 servings

per serving: 240 calories, 20 g protein, 28 g carbohydrates, 6 g total fat, 37 mg cholesterol, 184 mg sodium

lemon shrimp over caper couscous

preparation time: about 35 minutes

1 pound large raw shrimp (31 to 35 per lb.), shelled and deveined

2 cloves garlic, minced or pressed (optional)

³/₄ teaspoon chopped fresh oregano or ¹/₄ teaspoon dried oregano

¹/₂ teaspoon grated lemon peel

¹/₈ teaspoon pepper

2 tablespoons dry sherry

1 tablespoon cornstarch

2 cups fat-free reduced-sodium chicken broth

8 ounces asparagus

1 medium-size red bell pepper

1 cup couscous

2 tablespoons seasoned rice vinegar (or 2 tablespoons distilled white vinegar plus 3 teaspoon sugar)

1 to 2 tablespoons drained capers

1 tablespoon olive oil

Lemon wedges and oregano sprigs

1 In a large bowl, mix shrimp, garlic (if used) chopped oregano, ¹/₄ teaspoon of the lemon peel, and pepper. Set aside; stir occasionally.

2 To prepare sauce, in a small bowl, combine sherry and cornstarch; stir until blended. Stir in ¹/₂ cup of the broth; set aside.

3 Snap off and discard tough ends of asparagus; cut spears into ¹/₂-inch diagonal slices and set aside. Seed bell pepper, cut into thin strips, and set aside.

4 In a 3- to 4-quart pan, combine remaining 1¹/₂ cups broth and remaining ¹/₄ teaspoon lemon peel. Bring to a boil over high heat; stir in couscous. Cover, remove from heat, and let stand until liquid has been absorbed (about 5 minutes). Stir in vinegar and capers. Keep couscous warm; fluff occasionally with a fork.

5 In a wide nonstick frying pan or wok, combine asparagus, bell pepper, and ¹/₃ cup water. Cover and cook over medium-high heat until asparagus is almost tender to bite (about 3 minutes). Uncover and stir-fry until liquid has evaporated. Remove vegetables from pan and set aside.

6 Heat oil in pan. When oil is hot, add shrimp mixture and stir-fry for 2 minutes. Stir sauce well and pour into pan; then return asparagus and bell pepper to pan. Cook, stirring, until sauce boils and thickens slightly and shrimp are just opaque in center; cut to test (1 to 2 more minutes). Remove from heat.

7 To serve, spoon couscous onto a rimmed platter; top with shrimp mixture. Offer lemon wedges to squeeze to taste; garnish with oregano sprigs.

makes 4 servings

per serving: 355 calories, 28 g protein, 46 g carbohydrates, 5 g total fat, 140 mg cholesterol, 696 mg sodium

cool yogurt sauce

preparation time: about 5 minutes

1 cup plain nonfat yogurt

1 tablespoon *each* chopped fresh mint and cilantro

Salt

Fresh mint and cilantro leaves (optional)

In a small bowl, stir together yogurt, chopped mint, and chopped cilantro. Season to taste with salt. If made ahead, cover and refrigerate for up to 4 hours; stir before serving. Sprinkle with mint and cilantro leaves just before serving, if desired. Serve with cold poached or grilled salmon.

makes about 1 cup

per tablespoon: 8 calories, 0.8 g protein, 1 g carbohydrates, 0 g total fat, 0.3 mg cholesterol, 11 mg sodium

fish & fennel stew

preparation time: about 1 hour

1 large head fennel

1 tablespoon olive oil

1 large onion, chopped

6 cloves garlic, minced

1 1/4 pounds pear-shaped (Roma-type) tomatoes, chopped

2 cups fat-free reduced sodium chicken broth

1 bottle (about 8 oz.) clam juice

1/2 cup dry white wine

1/4 to 1/2 teaspoon ground red pepper (cayenne)

1 1/2 pounds boneless, skinless firm-textured, light-fleshed fish, such as halibut, swordfish, or sea bass, cut into 1 1/2-inch chunks

1. Trim stems from fennel, reserving feathery green leaves. Trim and discard any bruised areas from fennel. Finely chop leaves and set aside; thinly slice fennel head.

2. Heat oil in a 5- to 6-quart pan over medium heat. Add sliced fennel, onion, and garlic; cook; stirring often, until onion is sweet tasting and all vegetables are browned (about 20 minutes). Add water, 1/4 cup at a time, if pan appears dry.

3. Add tomatoes, broth, clam juice, wine, and red pepper. Bring to a boil; then reduce heat, cover, and simmer for 10 minutes. Add fish, cover, and simmer until just opaque but still moist in thickest part; cut to test (about 5 minutes). Stir in fennel leaves.

makes 4 servings

per serving: 317 calories, 40 g protein, 16 g carbohydrates, 8 g total fat, 54 mg cholesterol, 628 mg sodium

salmon with vegetable crust

preparation time: about 45 minutes

Vegetable oil cooking spray

2 medium-size thin-skinned potatoes (about 12 oz. *total*), scrubbed and cut into 1/4-inch- wide wedges

1 ounce Neufchatel cheese, at room temperature

1/8 teaspoon *each* salt and pepper

3 tablespoons lemon juice

1/4 cup *each* grated carrot and chopped tomato

2 tablespoons thinly sliced green onion

1 tablespoon finely chopped parsley

2 salmon steaks, cut about 1 inch thick (about 6 oz. *each*)

1. Coat a 3- by 13-inch baking pan with cooking spray. Arrange potatoes in pan, leaving enough room for fish. Bake potatoes in a 400° oven for 20 minutes. Meanwhile, in a small bowl, mix cheese, salt, pepper, and 1 tablespoon of the lemon juice until smooth and fluffy. Stir in carrot, tomato, onion, and parsley.

2. Rinse fish, pat dry, and place in pan alongside potatoes; drizzle fish with remaining 2 tablespoons lemon juice. Mound cream cheese mixture over fish, spreading nearly to edges. Continue to bake until potatoes are tender when pierced and fish is just opaque but still moist in thickest part; cut to test (about 12 more minutes).

makes 2 servings

per serving: 409 calories, 35 g protein, 36 g carbohydrates, 14 g total fat, 93 mg cholesterol, 287 mg sodium

scallops & shells with lemon cream

preparation time: 35 minutes

2 ounces Neufchatel or cream cheese,
   at room temperature

2 teaspoons honey

1 teaspoon Dijon mustard

$1/2$ teaspoon grated lemon peel

1 pound sea scallops

8 ounces dried medium-size pasta shells

$3/4$ cup fat-free reduced-sodium chicken broth

$1/4$ cup finely chopped Italian or regular parsley

2 teaspoons dry white wine (or to taste)

$1/4$ cup grated Parmesan cheese

1 In a food processor or blender, whirl Neufchatel cheese, honey, mustard, and lemon peel until smooth; set aside. Rinse scallops and pat dry; cut into bite-size pieces, if desired. Set aside.

2 In a 4- to 5-quart pan, bring about 8 cups water to a boil over medium-high heat; stir in pasta and cook until just tender to bite (8 to 10 minutes); or cook pasta according to package directions. Drain well, transfer to a large serving bowl, and keep warm.

3 In a 3- to 4-quart pan, bring broth to a boil over high heat. Add scallops and cook until opaque in center; cut to test (1 to 2 minutes).

4 With a slotted spoon, transfer scallops to bowl with pasta; keep warm. Quickly pour scallop cooking liquid from pan into Neufchatel cheese mixture in food processor; whirl until smooth. With a spoon, stir in parsley and wine. Pour sauce over scallops and pasta; sprinkle with Parmesan cheese. Serve immediately.

makes 4 servings

per serving: 393 calories, 31 g protein, 49 g carbohydrates, 7 g total fat, 53 mg cholesterol, 509 mg sodium

SMOKED SEAFOOD: Though prized for their special flavor, smoked fish and shellfish are too often reserved just for special-occasion buffets. Remember that smoked seafood can enliven any meal; offer it with lemon wedges and crackers or bread as an appetizer, or sliver it into quiches, egg dishes, or pasta sauces. For a salad, serve sliced or flaked smoked fish on lettuce, topped with toasted almonds and a mustard vinaigrette. With the exception of canned products, smoked seafood is perishable and must be refrigerated or frozen. Consume refrigerated varieties within a few days or purchase (or soon after opening the package); use frozen products within 6 months.

stuffed trout

preparation time: about 55 minutes

Toasted Bread Cubes (directions follow)

2 tablespoons finely chopped parsley

$^1/_2$ cup thinly sliced green onions (including tops)

1 medium-size red or green bell pepper, stemmed, seeded, and finely chopped

$^1/_2$ cup dry white wine or low-sodium chicken broth

1 tablespoon melted margarine

Salt and freshly ground pepper

6 boned and butterflied whole trout (about 8 oz. each), rinsed and patted dry

Nonstick cooking spray or salad oil

About $^1/_4$ cup lemon juice

Parsley sprigs and lemon wedges (optional)

1 Prepare Toasted Bread Cubes. In a bowl, stir together bread cubes, chopped parsley, onions, bell pepper, wine, and margarine. Season to taste with salt and pepper. Lightly pack stuffing into cavities of fish; sew openings with heavy thread or close with wooden picks. (Wrap any extra stuffing in foil and bake in pan alongside fish.)

2 Lightly coat a 9- by 13-inch baking pan with cooking spray. Add fish and brush with lemon juice. Cover and bake in a 400° oven for 10 minutes. Uncover and continue baking until fish looks just opaque but still moist in thickest part; cut to test (about 10 more minutes).

3 Transfer fish to a platter and remove thread. Garnish with parsley sprigs and lemon, if desired.

TOASTED BREAD CUBES

Cut about 6 ounces French or Italian bread into $^1/_2$-inch cubes (you should have about 4 cups). Spread in a single layer on a baking sheet and bake in a 400° oven until crisp (about 10 minutes).

makes 6 servings

per serving: 363 calories, 38 g protein, 18 g carbohydrates, 14 g total fat, 100 mg cholesterol, 279 mg sodium

dilled roughy in parchment

preparation time: about 35 minutes

1 tablespoon salad oil

3 tablespoons *each* white wine vinegar and chopped green onions (including tops)

1 teaspoon chopped fresh dill or $^1/_2$ teaspoon dry dill weed

1 teaspoon shredded tangerine or orange peel

1 large can (about 1 lb.) mandarin oranges, drained

Nonstick cooking spray

4 orange roughy fillets (about 5 oz. *each*), rinsed and patted, dry

1 Mix oil, vinegar, onions, dill, tangerine peel, and oranges. Set aside.

2 Cut 4 pieces of parchment paper, each about 4 times wider and 6 inches longer than each fish fillet. Coat each sheet with cooking spray, starting 1 inch from long side and covering an area the size of a fish fillet. Place a fillet on sprayed area of each sheet; spoon orange mixture over each fillet.

3 Fold long edge of parchment closest to fish over fish; then roll over several times to wrap fish in parchment. With seam side down, double fold each end, pressing lightly to crease and tucking ends under packet.

4 Place packets, folded ends underneath, slightly apart on a baking sheet; spray packets lightly with cooking spray. Bake in a 500° oven until fish looks just opaque but still moist in thickest part; cut a tiny slit through parchment into fish to test (7 to 10 minutes). Slash packets open and pull back parchment to reveal fish.

makes 4 servings

per serving: 283 calories, 21 g protein, 19 g carbohydrates, 14 g total fat, 28 mg cholesterol, 97 mg sodium

swordfish with mushroom sauce

preparation time: about 25 minutes
marinating time: 30 minutes

2 pounds swordfish or shark steaks, rinsed
    and patted dry

6 tablespoons lemon juice, 1 cup dry white wine
    or water

1 clove garlic, minced or pressed

1/2 teaspoon *each* dry oregano leaves, salt,
    and pepper

1/4 teaspoon fennel seeds, crushed

Nonstick cooking spray

1/2 pound mushrooms, sliced

2 teaspoon salad oil

1/2 cup thinly sliced green onions (including tops)

3 cups watercress sprigs

1 Cut fish into serving-size pieces, if necessary. In a 9- by 13-inch baking pan, stir together lemon juice, wine, garlic, oregano, salt, pepper, and fennel seeds. Add fish and let stand, turning occasionally, for 30 minutes. Lift out fish and drain briefly, reserving marinade.

2 Lightly coat a broiler pan rack with cooking spray. Place fish on rack and broil 3 to 4 inches below heat, turning once or twice, until fish looks just opaque but still moist in center; cut to test (8 to 10 minutes total).

3 Meanwhile, combine mushrooms and oil in a nonstick frying pan over medium-high heat. Cook, stirring, until mushrooms are soft (about 5 minutes). Stir in reserved marinade and boil gently for 2 minutes; stir in onions and remove from heat.

4 Arrange watercress on individual plates. Add fish and top with mushroom sauce.

makes 6 servings

per serving: 210 calories, 31 g protein, 4 g carbohydrates, 7 g total fat, 59 mg cholesterol, 332 mg sodium

chinese-style steamed fish

preparation time: about 35 minutes

1 scaled and cleaned whole rockfish, snapper, or
    black sea bass (about 2 lbs.), head removed,
    if desired, rinsed, and patted dry

Salt

3 tablespoons slivered fresh ginger

3 green onions (including tops), thinly sliced
    lengthwise

1 dried hot red chile

1 tablespoon unseasoned rice vinegar
    or wine vinegar

1 tablespoon reduced-sodium soy sauce

Cilantro sprigs (optional)

1 Make 3 diagonal slashes across fish on each side. Place on a rimmed plate that will fit on a steamer rack in a pan. (If fish is too long, cut in half crosswise and place halves side by side.) Season to taste with salt. Place half the ginger and onions inside cavity; put chile and remaining ginger and onions on top. Pour vinegar and soy sauce over fish.

2 Loosely cover with foil and place plate on a rack in a pan above 1 inch boiling water. Cover and steam until fish looks just opaque but still moist in thickest part; cut to test (8 to 10 minutes per inch of thickness).

3 Arrange fish on a large platter (reassemble halves, if necessary). Garnish with cilantro, if desired. To serve, cut through fish to backbone and slide a spatula between flesh and ribs to lift off each serving. Remove backbone to serve bottom half.

makes 4 servings

per serving: 170 calories, 32 g protein, 2 g carbohydrates, 3 g total fat, 60 mg cholesterol, 254 mg sodium

scallop scampi

preparation time: about 30 minutes

1 slice sourdough sandwich bread, torn into pieces

2 teaspoons olive oil

4 cloves garlic, minced or pressed

1 tablespoon chopped parsley

2 tablespoons dry white wine

1 teaspoon lemon juice

1/2 teaspoon honey

1 bunch watercress, coarse stems removed, sprigs rinsed and crisped

1 pound sea scallops

1 1/2 teaspoons butter or margarine

Lemon wedges

1 To prepare stir-fried crumbs, whirl bread in a blender or food processor to make fine crumbs. In a wide nonstick frying pan or wok, combine crumbs, 1 1/2 teaspoons water, 1/2 teaspoon of the olive oil, and a fourth of the garlic. Stir-fry over medium heat until crumbs are crisp and golden (about 5 minutes); remove from pan and set aside.

2 Let crumbs cool slightly. Stir parsley into crumbs and set aside.

3 In a small bowl, stir together wine, lemon juice, and honey; set aside. Arrange watercress on a large rimmed platter; cover and set aside.

4 Rinse scallops and pat dry; cut into bite-size pieces, if desired. Melt butter in remaining 1 1/2 teaspoons oil in a wide nonstick frying pan or wok over medium-high heat. When butter mixture is hot, add remaining garlic, 1 tablespoon water, and the scallops. Stir-fry until scallops are just opaque in center.

5 Stir wine mixture well and pour into pan; bring just to a boil. With a slotted spoon, lift scallops from pan; arrange over watercress. Pour pan juices into a small pitcher. Sprinkle scallops with stir-fried crumbs and garnish with lemon wedges.

makes 4 servings

per serving: 168 calories, 21 g protein, 9 g carbohydrates, 5 g total fat, 41 mg cholesterol, 257 mg sodium

red snapper stir-fry

preparation time: about 30 minutes

1 tablespoon finely minced fresh ginger

2 tablespoons reduced sodium soy sauce

2 tablespoons unsweetened pineapple juice

2 cloves garlic, minced or pressed

1 teaspoon sugar

1 teaspoon Asian sesame oil

1/8 teaspoon crushed red pepper flakes

1 pound red snapper fillets, cut into 1-inch pieces

1 medium-size pineapple

1 teaspoon vegetable oil

1 1/2 cups fresh Chinese pea pods

1 tablespoon cornstarch blended with 1 tablespoon cold water

1/2 cup thinly sliced green onions

1 In a large bowl, stir together ginger, soy sauce, pineapple juice, garlic, sugar, sesame oil, and red pepper flakes. Add fish and stir to coat. Set aside; stir occasionally.

2 Peel and core pineapple, then cut crosswise into thin slices. Arrange slices on a rimmed platter; cover and set aside.

3 Heat vegetable oil in a wide nonstick frying pan or wok over medium-high heat. When oil is hot, add fish mixture and stir-fry gently until fish is just opaque but still moist in thickest part; cut to test (2 to 3 minutes). Remove fish from pan with a slotted spoon; keep warm.

4 Add pea pods to pan and stir-fry for 30 seconds (15 seconds if using frozen pea pods). Stir cornstarch mixture well, then pour into pan. Cook, stirring constantly, until sauce boils and thickens slightly (1 to 2 minutes). Return fish to pan and add onions; mix gently but thoroughly, just until fish is hot and coated with sauce. To serve, spoon fish mixture over pineapple slices.

makes 4 servings

per serving: 278 calories, 26 g protein, 34 g carbohydrates, 5 g total fat, 42 mg cholesterol, 379 mg sodium

shrimp fajitas

preparation time: about 55 minutes

1 pound medium-size shrimp (about 35 *total*), shelled and deveined

1 cup lightly packed chopped cilantro

1 clove garlic, minced or pressed

1/3 cup lime juice

4 to 6 flour tortillas

1 tablespoon salad oil

2 large green bell peppers, stemmed, seeded, and thinly sliced

1 large onion, thinly sliced

1/2 cup plain nonfat yogurt

Bottled green tomatillo salsa

1 Stir together shrimp, cilantro, garlic, and lime juice. Let stand at room temperature for 20 minutes.

2 Meanwhile, wrap tortillas in foil and place in a 350° oven until hot (about 15 minutes).

3 Heat oil in a wide nonstick frying pan over medium-high heat. Add bell peppers and onion. Cook, stirring occasionally, until limp (about 10 minutes). Remove vegetables and keep warm. Add shrimp mixture to pan, increase heat to high, and cook, stirring often, until shrimp are opaque in center; cut to test (about 3 minutes). Return vegetables to pan, stirring to mix with shrimp.

4 Spoon shrimp mixture into tortillas, top with yogurt, and roll up. Offer with salsa.

makes 4 to 6 servings

per serving: 220 calories, 17 g protein, 28 g carbohydrates, 4 g total fat, 94 mg cholesterol, 285 mg sodium

shellfish couscous

preparation time: about 45 minutes

3 slices bacon, chopped

3/4 pound large shrimp (about 18 *total*), shelled and deveined

3/4 pound bay scallops, rinsed and patted dry

1 cup dry vermouth

2 1/2 cups low-sodium chicken broth

1/2 cup orange juice

2 cups couscous

1/4 cup dried tomatoes packed in oil, drained, rinsed, and slivered

2/3 cup minced chives

2 large oranges, thinly sliced

1 In a 4- to 5-quart pan, cook bacon over medium heat, stirring often, until crisp (about 7 minutes). Discard all but 2 tablespoons of the drippings from pan. Increase heat to medium-high and add shrimp and scallops. Cook, stirring often, until opaque in center; cut to test (about 5 minutes). Lift out shellfish and bacon; keep warm.

2 Add vermouth to pan; increase heat to high and boil until reduced by about half (about 5 minutes). Add chicken broth and orange juice. Bring to a boil; stir in couscous, tomatoes, and 1/3 cup of the chives. Cover, remove from heat, and let stand until liquid is absorbed (about 5 minutes).

3 Mound couscous on a platter and top with shellfish and bacon; sprinkle with remaining chives. Tuck oranges around couscous.

makes 6 servings

per serving: 484 calories, 30 g protein, 66 g carbohydrates, 10 g total fat, 94 mg cholesterol, 477 mg sodium

margarita shrimp

preparation time: about 25 minutes

1/4 cup gold or white tequila

1/2 teaspoon grated lime peel

2 tablespoons *each* lime juice and water

2 tablespoons minced cilantro or parsley

1 tablespoon honey

1/8 teaspoon white pepper

1 pound large shrimp (about 25 per lb.), shelled and deveined

About 2 teaspoons orange-flavored liqueur, or to taste

2 large red onions

Salt

Cilantro sprigs

Lime wedges

1 In a nonmetal bowl, mix tequila, lime peel, lime juice, water, minced cilantro, honey, and white pepper.

2 Pour tequila mixture into a wide nonstick frying pan. Add shrimp and cook over medium-high heat, stirring, until shrimp are just opaque but still moist in center; cut to test (3 to 4 minutes). With a slotted spoon, transfer shrimp to a bowl and keep warm. Bring cooking liquid to a boil over high heat; boil until reduced to 1/3 cup. Remove pan from heat; stir in liqueur, if desired.

3 While cooking liquid is boiling, thinly slice onions. Arrange onion slices in a single layer on a rimmed platter. To serve, spoon shrimp and cooking liquid over onion slices. Season to taste with salt; garnish with cilantro sprigs and lime wedges.

makes 4 servings

per serving: 173 calories, 21 g protein, 19 g carbohydrates, 2 g total fat, 140 mg cholesterol, 153 mg sodium

fish & clams in black bean sauce

preparation time: about 20 minutes

1 pound rockfish fillets

1 1/2 tablespoons fermented salted black beans, rinsed and drained

2 cloves garlic, minced or pressed

1 tablespoon reduced-sodium soy sauce

2 tablespoons dry sherry

3 green onions

3 thin slices fresh ginger

12 small hard-shell clams in shell, scrubbed

1 tablespoon salad oil

1 Rinse fish, pat dry, and place in a heatproof, 1-inch deep non-metal dish that is at least 1/2 inch smaller in diameter than the pan you will use for steaming.

2 In a small bowl, mash black beans with garlic; stir in soy sauce and sherry. Drizzle mixture over fish. Cut one of the onions into thirds; place cut onion and ginger on top of fish. Cut remaining 2 onions into 2-inch lengths; then cut lengths into thin shreds and set aside. Arrange clams around fish.

3 Set dish on a rack in a pan above about 1 inch of boiling water. Cover and steam, keeping water at a steady boil, until fish is just opaque but still moist in thickest part; cut to test (about 5 minutes). If fish is done before clams pop open, remove fish and continue to cook clams for a few more minutes, until shells pop open; then return fish to dish.

4 Using thick potholders, lift dish from pan. Remove and discard ginger and onion pieces, then sprinkle onion slivers over fish. Heat oil in a small pan until it ripples when pan is tilted; pour over fish (oil will sizzle). Before serving, discard any unopened clams.

makes 2 servings

per serving: 365 calories, 52 g protein, 7 g carbohydrates, 12 g total fat, 98 mg cholesterol, 799 mg sodium

couscous with berries & shrimp

preparation time: about 30 minutes

1 package (about 10 oz.) couscous

1 small cucumber

1 cup firmly packed fresh mint leaves

1/2 cup lemon juice

2 tablespoons olive oil

About 1/2 teaspoon honey (or to taste)

1 cup fresh blueberries or other fresh berries

Salt and pepper

4 to 8 large lettuce leaves, rinsed and crisped

6 to 8 ounces small cooked shrimp

Lemon wedges and mint sprigs

1 In a 2 1/2- to 3-quart pan, bring 2 1/4 cups water to a boil over medium-high heat. Stir in couscous; cover, remove from heat, and let stand until liquid has been absorbed (about 5 minutes). Then transfer couscous to a large bowl and let stand until cool (about 10 minutes), fluffing often with a fork.

2 Meanwhile, peel, halve, and seed cucumber; thinly slice halves and set aside. Finely chop mint leaves, place in a small bowl, and mix in lemon juice, oil, and honey. Add cucumber and blueberries to couscous; then add mint dressing and mix gently but thoroughly. Season to taste with salt and pepper.

3 Line each of 4 individual plates with 1 or 2 lettuce leaves. Mound couscous mixture in center of each plate; top with shrimp. Garnish with lemon wedges and mint sprigs.

makes 4 servings

per serving: 419 calories, 21 g protein, 66 g carbohydrates, 8 g total fat, 97 mg cholesterol, 129 mg sodium

orange roughy with polenta

preparation time: about 30 minutes

1 cup polenta

4 1/3 cups low-sodium chicken broth

1/2 teaspoon cumin seeds

1 large can (about 7 oz.) diced green chiles

1 pound orange roughy fillets, cut into 4 equal pieces

1 medium-size red bell pepper, seeded and minced

1 tablespoon cilantro leaves

Salt

Lime wedges

1 Pour polenta into a 3- to 4-quart pan; stir in broth and cumin seeds. Bring to a boil over high heat, stirring often with a long-handled wooden spoon (mixture will spatter). Reduce heat and simmer gently, uncovered, stirring often, until polenta tastes creamy (about 20 minutes). Stir in chiles.

2 While polenta is simmering, rinse fish and pat dry; then arrange in a 9- by 13-inch baking pan. Bake in a 475° oven until fish is just opaque but still moist in thickest part; cut to test (about 6 minutes).

3 To serve, spoon polenta onto 4 individual plates. Top each serving with a piece of fish; sprinkle with bell pepper and cilantro. Season to taste with salt; serve with lime wedges.

makes 4 servings

per serving: 326 calories, 23 g protein, 34 g carbohydrates, 10 g total fat, 23 mg cholesterol, 434 mg sodium

lingcod with citrus almond couscous

preparation time: about 50 minutes

5 or 6 small oranges (about 2 ½ lbs. total)

1 large pink grapefruit

1 medium-size lemon

1 medium-size lime

¼ cup slivered almonds

2 tablespoons olive oil

¼ cup chopped onion

½ teaspoon almond extract

10 ounces dried couscous

2 pounds skinless, boneless lingcod or striped bass fillets (*each* about 1 inch thick)

½ cup rice vinegar

2 tablespoons minced shallots

1 Shred enough peel from oranges and grapefruit to make 1½ tablespoons each. Shred enough peel from lemon and lime to make 1 teaspoon each. Combine peels in a small bowl; set aside. Remove remaining peel and white membrane from grapefruit, lemon, lime, and 2 of the oranges. Over a bowl, cut between membranes to release segments. In a separate bowl, juice remaining oranges to make 1½ cups. Set bowls aside.

2 Toast almonds in a 2- to 3-quart pan over medium heat, shaking pan often, until golden (about 4 minutes). Remove from pan and set aside. Place 2 teaspoons of the oil in pan and heat over medium-high heat. Add onion and cook, stirring often, until soft (about 3 minutes). Add 1 cup of the orange juice, 1½ cups water, and almond extract. Bring to a boil. Stir in pasta; cover, remove from heat, and let stand until liquid is absorbed (about 5 minutes). Keep warm, fluffing occasionally with a fork.

3 Cut fish into 6 portions and brush with 2 teaspoons more oil. Place on rack of a 12- by 14-inch broiler pan. Broil about 4 inches below heat, turning once, just until opaque but still moist in thickest part; cut to test (about 10 minutes).

4 Combine remaining ½ cup orange juice and 2 teaspoons oil, vinegar, shallots, fruit, and accumulated juices in a wide nonstick frying pan. Cook over medium heat, stirring often, until warm (about 2 minutes).

5 Arrange pasta and fish on individual plates. Top fish with fruit sauce and sprinkle almonds over pasta. Garnish with citrus peel.

makes 6 servings

per serving: 455 calories, 35 g protein, 57 g carbohydrates, 10 g total fat, 79 mg cholesterol, 97 mg sodium

garlic shrimp with rice

preparation time: about 25 minutes

2 teaspoons butter or margarine

2 teaspoons olive oil

3 cloves garlic, minced or pressed

1 pound large shrimp (about 25 per lb.), shelled and deveined

About 4 cups hot cooked rice

Lemon wedges

1 Melt butter in a wide nonstick frying pan over medium-high heat.

2 Add oil, garlic, 3 tablespoons water, and shrimp. Cook, stirring, until shrimp are just opaque but still moist in center; cut to test (3 to 4 minutes).

3 To serve, spoon rice onto a platter or 4 dinner plates; Spoon shrimp and pan juices over rice. Sprinkle with parsley. Season to taste with salt and pepper, then serve with lemon wedges.

makes 4 servings

per serving: 403 calories, 24 g proteins, 59 g carbohydrates, 6 g total fat, 145 mg cholesterol, 161 mg sodium

balsamic-broiled salmon with mint

preparation time: about 40 minutes

1 1/4 pounds small red thin-skinned potatoes, scrubbed

3 tablespoons balsamic or raspberry vinegar

1 1/2 tablespoons honey

3/4 teaspoon vegetable oil

1 to 1 1/4 pounds salmon fillets (3/4 inch thick)

1/2 cup fresh mint leaves, minced

Mint sprigs

Lemon slices

1 Peel a 1-inch-wide strip around center of each potato. Steam potatoes, covered, on a rack above about 1 inch of boiling water until tender when pierced (about 25 minutes).

2 Meanwhile, in a small bowl, stir together vinegar, honey, and oil.

3 Remove and discard any skin from salmon; rinse salmon and pat dry. Cut salmon into 4 serving-size pieces; place, skinned sides down, in a lightly greased shallow rimmed baking pan. Drizzle salmon with half the vinegar mixture.

4 Broil about 6 inches below heat, brushing several times with remaining vinegar mixture, until just opaque but still moist in thickest part; cut to test (8 to 10 minutes).

5 Transfer salmon to a warm platter; drizzle with any cooking juices. Surround with potatoes. Sprinkle salmon and potatoes with minced mint; garnish with mint sprigs and lemon slices.

makes 4 servings

per serving: 332 calories, 28 g protein, 33 g carbohydrates, 9 g total fat, 71 mg cholesterol, 68 mg sodium

stir-fried tuna on spinach

preparation time: about 40 minutes

1/4 cup mirin or cream sherry

6 tablespoons unseasoned rice vinegar or cider vinegar

2 tablespoons reduced-sodium soy sauce

1 teaspoon prepared horseradish

3 quarts lightly packed rinsed, crisped spinach leaves

1 tablespoon sesame seeds

1 teaspoon vegetable oil

2 tablespoons finely minced fresh ginger

12 ounces fresh tuna, cut into 2- by 2-inch strips

1/2 cup thinly sliced green onions

1 cup thinly sliced red radishes

Whole green onions (ends trimmed)

1 To prepare soy dressing, in a small bowl, stir together mirin, vinegar, soy sauce, and horseradish; set aside.

2 Arrange spinach on a large platter, cover, and set aside.

3 In a wide nonstick frying pan or wok, stir sesame seeds over medium heat until golden (about 3 minutes). Pour out of pan and set aside.

4 Heat oil in pan over medium-high heat. When oil is hot, add ginger and stir-fry just until light brown (about 30 seconds; do not scorch). Add tuna and stir-fry gently (flipping with a spatula, if needed) until just opaque but still moist and pink in thickest part; cut to test (about 3 minutes). Stir soy dressing and pour into pan; stir to mix, then remove pan from heat.

5 Spoon tuna mixture over spinach on platter. Sprinkle with sliced green onions, radishes, and sesame seeds. Garnish with whole green onions.

makes 4 servings

per serving: 220 calories , 24 g protein, 12 g carbohydrates, 7 g total fat, 32 mg cholesterol, 411 mg sodium

tuna & cherry tomato salsa

preparation time: about 25 minutes

1 pound red or yellow cherry tomatoes, chopped

$^1/_2$ cup lightly packed cilantro leaves, coarsely chopped

2 fresh jalapeño chiles, seeded and coarsely chopped

1 clove garlic, minced or pressed

3 green onions, thinly sliced

5 tablespoons lime juice

1 teaspoon olive oil

4 skinless, boneless tuna steaks (about 4 oz. *each*), $^3/_4$ to 1 inch thick

2 medium-size cucumbers, thinly sliced

Freshly ground pepper

In a medium-size bowl, mix tomatoes, cilantro, chiles, garlic, onions, and 2 tablespoons of the lime juice. Cover and set aside.

1 Mix remaining 3 tablespoons lime juice with oil. Rinse tuna and pat dry; then brush both sides of each steak with oil mixture. Place tuna on a greased grill 4 to 6 inches above a solid bed of hot coals. Cook, turning once, until browned on outside but still pale pink in the center; cut to test (about 3 minutes).

2 Transfer tuna to a warm platter; surround with cucumber slices. Evenly top tuna with tomato salsa; season to taste with pepper.

makes 4 servings

per serving: 225 calories, 29 g protein, 12 g carbohydrates, 7 g total fat, 43 mg cholesterol, 64 mg sodium

seed-crusted fish, indian style

preparation time: about 15 minutes

1 teaspoon *each* coriander seeds and mustard seeds

$^1/_2$ teaspoon *each* coarsely ground pepper, cumin seeds, and fennel seeds

1 pound lingcod, rockfish, or orange roughy fillets ($^1/_2$ to 1 inch thick)

2 teaspoons salad oil

Cilantro sprigs

1 Mix coriander seeds, mustard seeds, pepper, cumin seeds, and fennel seeds; set aside.

2 Rinse fish, pat dry, and cut into 4 equal pieces. Brush with oil and place on a rack in a 12- by 14-inch broiler pan. Broil about 3 inches below heat for 3 minutes. Turn fish over, sprinkle with seed mixture, and continue to broil until just opaque but still moist in thickest part; cut to test (2 to 4 more minutes). Garnish with cilantro sprigs.

makes 4 servings

per serving: 125 calories, 20 g protein, 0.9 g carbohydrates, 4 g total fat, 59 mg cholesterol, 68 mg sodium

pink peppercorn swordfish

preparation time: 30 minutes

¼ **cup whole pink peppercorns**

4 **swordfish or halibut steaks (***each* **about 1-inch thick and 5 to 6 oz.)**

8 **teaspoons honey**

4 **large butter lettuce leaves, rinsed and crisped**

2 **jars (about 6 oz.** *each***) marinated artichoke hearts, drained**

Lemon wedges

1 In a 1- to 1½-quart pan, combine peppercorns and about 2 cups water. Bring to a boil over high heat; then reduce heat and simmer until peppercorns are slightly softened (about 4 minutes). Drain well.

2 Rinse fish and pat dry. Arrange pieces well apart in a lightly oiled shallow 10- by 15-inch baking pan. Brush each piece with 2 teaspoons of the honey; then top equally with peppercorns, spreading them in a single layer.

3 Bake in a 400° oven until fish is just opaque but still moist in thickest part; cut to test (about 10 minutes).

4 Place one lettuce leaf on each of 4 individual plates; top lettuce with artichokes. With a wide spatula, lift fish from baking pan and arrange alongside lettuce. Season to taste with lemon.

makes 4 servings

per serving: 277 calories, 30 g protein, 21 g carbohydrates, 9 g total fat, 54 mg cholesterol, 361 mg sodium

snapper veracruz

preparation time: about 35 minutes

1 **teaspoon salad oil or olive oil**

1 **small green or red bell pepper, seeded and chopped**

1 **large onion, chopped**

3 **cloves garlic, minced or pressed (optional)**

2 **tablespoons water**

1 **small can (about 4 oz.) diced green chiles**

¼ **cup sliced pimiento-stuffed green olives**

3 **tablespoons lime juice**

1 **teaspoon ground cinnamon**

¼ **teaspoon white pepper**

1 **can (about 14 ½ oz.) stewed tomatoes**

4 **snapper or rockfish fillets (about 2 lbs. total)**

1 **tablespoon drained capers**

1 Heat oil in a wide nonstick frying pan over medium-high heat. Add bell pepper, onion, garlic (if desired), and water; cook, stirring often, until vegetables are tender-crisp to bite (3 to 5 minutes).

2 Add chiles, olives, lime juice, cinnamon, and white pepper; cook for 1 more minute. Add tomatoes to pan (break tomatoes up with a spoon, if needed); then bring mixture to a boil. Boil, stirring often, until sauce is slightly thickened (about 5 minutes).

3 Rinse fish, pat dry, and arrange in a lightly greased 9- by 13-inch baking dish. Pour sauce over fish. Bake in a 350° oven until fish is just opaque but still moist in thickest part; cut to test (10 to 15 minutes).

4 With a slotted spoon, transfer fish and sauce to four dinner plates. Sprinkle with capers.

makes 4 servings

per serving: 310 calories, 49 g protein, 16 g carbohydrates, 16 g total fat, 84 mg cholesterol, 842 mg sodium

artichokes with shrimp & cilantro salsa

preparation time: about 1 hour

1/2 cup seasoned rise vinegar; or 1/2 cup distilled white vinegar plus 1 tablespoon sugar

1 tablespoon mustard seeds

1 teaspoon whole black peppercorns

4 thin quarter-size slices fresh ginger

3 large artichokes, *each* 4 to 4 1/2 inches in diameter

12 ounces tiny cooked shrimp

1/3 cup minced pickled scallions

1/4 cup minced cilantro

1/4 cup minced fresh mint or 1 tablespoon dried mint

2 tablespoons reduced-sodium soy sauce

1/4 to 1/2 teaspoon chili oil

Mint or cilantro sprigs

1 In a 6- to 8-quart pan, combine 1/4 cup of the vinegar, mustard seeds, peppercorns, ginger, and 4 quarts water. Cover and bring to a boil over high heat.

2 Meanwhile, remove coarse outer leaves from artichokes and trim stems flush with bases. Cut off top third of each artichoke. Trim thorny tips from remaining leaves. Immerse artichokes in cold water to clean and shake to drain.

3 Lower artichokes into boiling vinegar-water mixture. Then reduce heat and simmer, covered, until artichoke bottoms are tender when pierced (about 35 minutes). Drain, reserving cooking liquid. Let artichokes stand until they are cool enough to handle.

4 Pour artichoke-cooking liquid through a fine strainer set over a bowl; discard ginger and reserve mustard seeds and peppercorns. Place shrimp in strainer. Rinse shrimp with cool water; then drain well, place in a bowl, and mix with reserved seasoning, remaining 1/4 cup vinegar, scallions, minced cilantro, minced mint, soy sauce, and chili oil.

5 Cut each artichoke in half lengthwise. Remove inner leaves and scoop out fuzzy centers. Set each artichoke half on a plate. Spoon shrimp mixture into artichokes; garnish with mint sprigs.

makes 6 servings

per serving: 122 calories, 15 g protein, 13 g carbohydrates, 2 g total fat, 111 mg cholesterol, 911 mg sodium

mussels provencal

preparation time: about 45 minutes

3 1/2 pounds mussels in shell, scrubbed

1 tablespoon olive oil

3 cloves garlic, minced or pressed

1 large onion, chopped

1 cup chopped celery

1 large can (about 28 oz.) tomatoes

1 cup dry white wine or low-sodium chicken broth

1/2 cup minced parsley

1/2 teaspoon pepper

1 Pull beard from each mussel with a swift tug. Set mussels aside.

2 Heat oil in a 6- to 8-quart pan over medium-high heat. Add garlic, onion, and celery. Cook, stirring often, until vegetables are soft (about 7 minutes). Cut up tomatoes; then add tomatoes and their liquid to pan. Bring to a boil; then reduce heat, cover, and simmer for 15 minutes. Add wine, parsley, and pepper. Cover and bring to a boil.

3 Add mussels, cover, and cook until shells pop open (7 to 9 minutes). Discard any unopened mussels. With a slotted spoon, transfer mussels to wide, shallow bowls; ladle sauce over each serving.

makes 4 to 6 servings

per serving: 194 calories, 13 g protein, 17 g carbohydrates, 5 g total fat, 26 mg cholesterol, 551 mg sodium

tuna steaks with roasted peppers & tuna sauce

preparation time: about 55 minutes

5 ½ cups fat-free reduced-sodium chicken broth

½ cup finely chopped dried apricots

1 pound dried orzo or other tiny rice-shaped pasta

1 can (about 6 ⅛ oz.) tuna packed in water

1 large egg yolk or 1 tablespoon pasteurized egg substitute

¼ teaspoon grated lemon peel

2 tablespoons lemon juice

4 teaspoons balsamic vinegar

1 teaspoon honey

½ teaspoon Dijon mustard

½ teaspoon salt (or to taste)

¼ cup *each* olive oil and salad oil

3 canned anchovy fillets, drained

1 cup nonfat sour cream

2 tablespoons fennel seeds

1 tablespoon whole white peppercorns

1 ½ teaspoons coriander seeds

2 large egg whites

4 tuna (ahi) steaks (*each* about 1 inch thick and about 7 oz.)

1 teaspoon olive oil

½ cup bottled clam juice

1 jar roasted red peppers (about 12 oz.), drained and patted dry

3 tablespoons drained capers (or to taste)

Lemon slices

Italian or regular parsley sprigs

1 In a 4- to 5-quart pan, bring broth and apricots to a boil over high heat; stir in orzo. Reduce heat, cover, and simmer, stirring occasionally, until almost all liquid has been absorbed (about 20 minutes); as liquid cooks down, stir more often and watch closely to prevent scorching. Remove from heat and keep warm.

2 While orzo is cooking, drain can of tuna, reserving ¼ cup of the liquid from can. Set tuna and liquid aside.

3 In a food processor or blender, combine egg yolk, lemon peel, lemon juice, vinegar, honey, mustard, and ¼ teaspoon of the salt (or to taste); whirl until blended. With motor running, slowly pour in the ¼ cup olive oil and salad oil in a thin, steady stream. Whirl until well blended. Add canned tuna, reserved tuna liquid, 1 tablespoon water, and anchovies; whirl until smoothly pureed. With a spoon or whisk, stir in sour cream; set aside.

4 Wash and dry food processor or blender; then combine fennel seeds, peppercorns, coriander seeds, and remaining ¼ teaspoon salt in processor or blender. Whirl until finely ground; transfer to a wide, shallow bowl. In another wide, shallow bowl, beat egg whites to blend. Rinse tuna steaks and pat dry; then cut each in half. Dip pieces, one at a time, in egg whites; drain briefly, then coat on both sides with seed mixture. Pat any remaining seed mixture on fish.

5 Heat the 1 teaspoon olive oil in a wide nonstick frying pan over medium-high heat. Add fish and cook, turning once, until browned on both sides. Add clam juice. Reduce heat and cook until fish is still pale pink in center; cut to test (about 5 minutes).

6 Spoon pasta onto a rimmed platter; fluff with a fork. With a slotted spoon, lift fish from pan and place atop pasta; arrange red peppers decoratively around fish. Top with half the tuna sauce and sprinkle with capers. Garnish with lemon slices and parsley sprigs. Offer remaining tuna sauce to add to taste.

makes 8 servings

per serving: 562 calories, 39 g protein, 60 g carbohydrates, 18 g total fat, 77 mg cholesterol, 1,201 mg sodium

index